UNDERSTANDING
PHILIP ROTH

UNDERSTANDING CONTEMPORARY AMERICAN LITERATURE
Matthew J. Bruccoli, Founding Editor
Linda Wagner-Martin, Series Editor

Also of Interest

UNDERSTANDING

PHILIP ROTH

Matthew A. Shipe

THE UNIVERSITY OF
SOUTH CAROLINA PRESS

© 2022 University of South Carolina

Published by the University of South Carolina Press
Columbia, South Carolina 29208

www.uscpress.com

Manufactured in the United States of America

31 30 29 28 27 26 25 24 23 22
10 9 8 7 6 5 4 3 2 1

Library of Congress Cataloging-in-Publication Data
can be found at http://catalog.loc.gov/.

ISBN 978-1-64336-309-7 (hardcover)
ISBN 978-1-64336-310-3 (paperback)
ISBN 978-1-64336-311-0 (ebook)

To Dylan, Lucas, and Hallie

CONTENTS

SERIES EDITOR'S PREFACE

The Understanding Contemporary American Literature series was founded by the estimable Matthew J. Bruccoli (1931–2008), who envisioned these volumes as guides or companions for students as well as good nonacademic readers, a legacy that will continue as new volumes are developed to fill in gaps among the nearly one hundred series volumes published to date and to embrace a host of new writers only now making their marks on our literature.

As Professor Bruccoli explained in his preface to the volumes he edited, because much influential contemporary literature makes special demands, "the word *understanding* in the titles was chosen deliberately. Many willing readers lack an adequate understanding of how contemporary literature works; that is, of what the author is attempting to express and the means by which it is conveyed." Aimed at fostering this understanding of good literature and good writers, the criticism and analysis in the series provide instruction in how to read certain contemporary writers—explicating their material, language, structures, themes, and perspectives—and facilitate a more profitable experience of the works under discussion.

In the twenty-first century Professor Bruccoli's prescience gives us an avenue to publish expert critiques of significant contemporary American writing. The series continues to map the literary landscape and to provide both instruction and enjoyment. Future volumes will seek to introduce new voices alongside canonized favorites, to chronicle the changing literature of our times, and to remain, as Professor Bruccoli conceived, contemporary in the best sense of the word.

Linda Wagner-Martin, Series Editor

ACKNOWLEDGMENTS

Writing this book during the middle of a pandemic was not what I had imagined when I first proposed it, but I greatly appreciate everyone who has helped me during these past eighteen months. This book would not exist if it weren't for the enthusiasm of Richard Brown, Linda Wagner-Martin, and Aurora Bell. It's been a pleasure to work with everyone at the University of South Carolina Press, but I would especially like to thank Aurora for all she has done to help bring this book to fruition. A big thank you goes out to Robert Milder, Ernie Shipe, and James Williams for reading earlier versions of this book. Their insight and intelligence have made this a much stronger work. I'd also like to acknowledge my friends in the Roth Society—especially Jacques Berlinerblau, Jim Bloom, Andy Connolly, Louis Gordon, Maggie McKinley, Ira Nadel, Aimee Pozorski, and Debra Shostak—all of whom were kind of enough to answer my questions and share their expertise. Reading the work of my fellow Roth scholars has also been a pleasure, but I'd like to especially acknowledge Murray Baumgarten and Barbara Gottfried's original volume on Roth for this series. I'd like to thank my colleagues in the English Department at Washington University in St. Louis for their support during the writing of this book. Many of the ideas in the later chapters of this book were sharpened by having taught Roth to my undergraduate students in my "End of the Century" seminar. The intellectual energy and enthusiasm that they brought to our discussions was inspiring, and I'm grateful for having had the opportunity to discuss Roth with them. I'd also like to thank Marshall Boswell, in whose class I first read *American Pastoral* as a junior at Rhodes College—thanks for getting me hooked on Roth.

Finally, I'd like to thank my family for all their love and support during the writing of this book. Thanks to my parents, Betty and Ernie Shipe, for all they have given me through the years and for the free babysitting that allowed me to finish the book on time. Finally, this work wouldn't have been possible without my wife, Jaime, and our children, Dylan, Lucas, and Hallie (who kindly delayed her appearance until right after the first draft of this book was completed).

A substantially revised section of chapter 1 originally appeared as the first chapter, "Life," in the edited collection *Philip Roth in Context*, edited by Maggie McKinley. Copyright © Cambridge University Press, 2021. Reprinted with permission.

CHAPTER 1

Understanding Philip Roth

With the 1959 publication of his debut, *Goodbye, Columbus and Five Short Stories,* Philip Milton Roth established himself as one of the most prominent and controversial American writers of his generation. Born in Newark, New Jersey, in 1933, Roth grew up in the secure confines of the largely Jewish Wee-quahic neighborhood of Newark, terrain that he would frequently revisit in his fiction. Over the course of a career that spanned five decades and thirty-one books, Roth chronicled the cultural and political changes that transformed the United States during the second half of the twentieth century. That said, Roth's great subject was in many ways himself—Nathan Zuckerman, one of several alter-egos who populate his fiction, is a Jewish American writer whose career and life mirror Roth's own—and his novels explicitly play with readers' inclination to confuse fiction for confession. In the concluding section of *The Facts: A Writer's Autobiography* (1988), Zuckerman writes a letter to his creator, advising Roth against publishing his memoir. "Your gift is not to personalize your experience but to personify it, to embody it in the representation of a person who is *not* yourself," Zuckerman admonishes Roth. "You are not an autobiographer, you're a personificator" (162). However, in rearranging and distorting the facts of his life into different fictional contortions, Roth made an argument for the necessity of the novel, his fiction capturing the exhausting and, at times, maddening nature of American life in the closing decades of the twentieth century.

Although the commercial success of his third novel, the sexually explicit *Portnoy's Complaint,* in 1969 made Roth a literary celebrity, it was his subsequent work, particularly that of his middle and later periods, that secured his legacy as one of the most significant American novelists of the post-1945 era. Beginning with *The Counterlife* (1986) and continuing through *The Plot Against America* (2004), Roth released a series of formally inventive and thematically ambitious novels that propelled his literary reputation, a sustained mid-career rejuvenation that, with the exception of Henry James, remains unmatched by that of any American novelist. While the Nobel Prize ultimately eluded him—of Bob Dylan's 2016 victory he quipped that "it's O.K., but next year I hope Peter, Paul and Mary get it"[1]—Roth concluded his career, alongside Toni Morrison, as perhaps the most accomplished American novelist of his generation, his late career success elevating him above John Updike and Saul Bellow, the two contemporaries with whom he was most frequently compared. By the time of his death in May 2018, Roth had won the Pulitzer Prize, two National Book Awards, and three PEN/Faulkner Awards. In 2005, he became only the third living writer to have his work published by the Library of America, and in 2011 he won the Man Booker International Prize.

Throughout his fifty-year career, Roth played with the form of the novel, displaying a dexterity and willingness to experiment that distinguished his fictional output. Summing up his achievement in the pages of the *New Yorker*, James Wood observed, "More than any other postwar American novelist, Roth wrote the self—the self was examined, cajoled, lampooned, fictionalized, ghosted, exalted, disgraced, but above all constituted by and in writing. Maybe you have to go back to the very different Henry James to find an American novelist so purely a bundle of words, so restlessly and absolutely committed to the investigation and construction of life through language."[2] Beginning his career as a traditional realist—his first novel, *Letting Go* (1962), remains deeply indebted to Henry James while its follow-up, *When She Was Good* (1967), displays an affinity for Theodore Dreiser and Sherwood Anderson—Roth quickly exploded the possibilities of the novel. Starting with *Portnoy's Complaint*, a work that transformed the psychoanalytic experience into an uninhibited (and obscene) stand-up routine, Roth liberated himself from the seriousness and traditional forms that had constrained his earlier fiction. "Sheer Playfulness and Deadly Seriousness are my closest friends; it is with them that I take my walk at the end of the day," Roth affirmed in a 1974 interview with Joyce Carol Oates (*Why Write?* 120). After *Portnoy's Complaint*, the narrative experiments would become bolder: novels such as *My Life as a Man* (1974), *The Counterlife*, and *Operation Shylock: A Confession* (1993) fully embrace the postmodern narrative experiments that are typically associated with metafictional writers such as John Barth, John Fowles, and Donald Barthelme. Indeed, Roth's impulse to play with different narrative forms would extend to his final novels, the narrative fragmentation that characterizes *Exit Ghost* (2007) and *Indignation* (2008) reflecting "the sense of apartness and exile and anachronism" that Edward Said theorizes as being essential to late style.[3]

For all his remarkable productivity and penchant for formal experimentation and innovation, Roth frequently circled around a firmly established series of concerns and themes in his fiction. Questions of Jewish American identity; the power struggle between fathers and sons; the irrationality of male sexual desire; the consequences of exercising one's (artistic, sexual, personal) freedom; the tumultuous history of Newark; the nature of the American experiment —these are the central concerns that percolate throughout his thirty-one books. In repeatedly revisiting these questions, reworking them from different perspectives and never settling on a simplistic or, for that matter, comprehensive answer to any of them, Roth constructed one of the richest bodies of work in American fiction, a corpus that grows in resonance when one realizes how later works such as *Indignation* and *Nemesis* (2010) revisit the themes that propelled his early fiction. By emphasizing the connections between his early and late work, *Understanding Philip Roth* attempts to show how Roth's fiction evolved over the course of a half-century. Additionally, this volume sets Roth's work in the context of the charges of misogyny and of being a self-hating Jew that were leveled against him throughout his career. Starting with *The Human Stain* (2000), Roth organized his corpus by narrative voice (e.g., "Philip Roth" and Nathan Zuckerman), and the chapters of this study, with a few exceptions, follow this grouping to illustrate how Roth's books speak to each other in a sort of endless conversational circle, each novel picking up themes and narrative strands featured in an earlier work.

From the conservatism of the Eisenhower years to the uncertainties of the post-9/11 world, Roth's novels offer a richly observed chronicle of this period of American life, his fiction capturing the absurdities, contradictions, and turmoil that shaped the US in the six decades following its ascendance as a world power after the Second World War. In "Writing American Fiction" (1960), an essay he published at the outset of his career, Roth quipped that the "American writer in the middle of the twentieth century has his hands full in trying to understand, describe, and then make *credible* much of American reality. It stupefies, it sickens, it infuriates, and finally it is even a kind of embarrassment to one's own meager imagination" (*Why Write?* 27). Such indignation frequently characterizes Roth's male protagonists' response to their political and cultural climate. In the opening section of *The Human Stain*, for example, Nathan Zuckerman reflects on the national uproar triggered by President Bill Clinton's affair with his much younger intern Monica Lewinsky, a scandal that consumed the American consciousness during the summer of 1998 and that resulted in Clinton's impeachment (he would subsequently be acquitted in the Senate):

It was the summer in America when the nausea returned, when the joking didn't stop, when the speculation and the theorizing and the hyperbole didn't stop, when the moral obligation to explain to one's children about adult life was abrogated in favor of maintaining in them every illusion about adult life, when the smallness of people was simply crushing, when some kind of demon had been unleashed in the nation and, on both sides, people wondered "Why are we so crazy?," when men and women alike, upon awakening in the morning, discovered that during the night, in a state of sleep that transported them beyond envy or loathing, they had dreamed of the brazenness of Bill Clinton. I myself dreamed of a mammoth banner, draped Dadaistically like a Christo wrapping from one end of the White House to the other and bearing a legend A HUMAN BEING LIVES HERE. It was the summer when—for the billionth time—the jumble, the mayhem, the mess proved itself more subtle than this one's ideology and that one's morality. It was the summer when a president's penis was on everyone's mind, and life, in its shameless impurity, once again confounded America. (3)

These breaks are, for Roth, an integral, even defining, aspect of the American experience, as recurrent as they are ultimately inexplicable. Throughout his career, Roth would return to the notion of a sinister or chthonic force periodically entering American life and contaminating our public imagination—what Zuckerman diagnoses in *American Pastoral* as "the indigenous American berserk" (86). It is a madness that counters what Roth describes in a 1973 self-interview as "the mythic" self-image that the United States has always struggled to maintain (*Reading Myself* 87). In a discussion of his 1973 baseball farce, *The Great American Novel*, Roth observed how he located "in baseball a means to dramatize the *struggle* between the benign national myth of itself that a great power prefers to perpetuate, and the relentlessly insidious, very nearly demonic reality (like the kind we had known in the sixties) that will not give an inch on behalf of that idealized mythology" (*Reading Myself* 89–90). In the American Trilogy especially (*American Pastoral, I Married a Communist* [1998], and *The Human Stain*), Roth illuminates how America's idealized vision of itself intensifies the pain, the destabilizing sense of loss and confusion that is an irreparable byproduct of the knowledge of the nightmarish proclivities that shadow, and at times *define*, our history. Such conflicts are, of course, not limited to the period that Roth lived through—they run throughout the United States' history. Nor are they a uniquely American phenomenon: Roth's fiction remains acutely aware of the violence that shaped the twentieth century, in particular the cataclysmic violence of the Holocaust. Roth's skeptical view of progress, however, should not be confused with political conservatism—Roth was an avowed Democrat throughout his life—or for a misguided nostalgia. When asked in a 2002 interview to comment on how the September 11, 2001, attacks had triggered a national loss of innocence, Roth retorted: "What innocence? That's so naïve. From 1668 to 1865 we had slavery in the country. Then, from 1865 to 1955, a society marked by brutal segregation. What innocence? I don't really know what people are talking about."[4]

In its emphasis on conflict and tension, Roth's fiction nevertheless recognizes the very real human desire for the pastoral and all the innocence and peace that the genre portends. It is a sense of harmony that captivates, but ultimately eludes, Roth's male protagonists. "But tranquility is disquieting to you, Nathan, in writing particularly—it's bad art to you, far too comfortable for the reader and certainly for yourself," Zuckerman's English wife, Maria, tells him toward the conclusion of *The Counterlife* in a letter announcing that she is leaving the novel.[5] "The last thing you want is to make readers happy, with everything cozy and strifeless, and desire simply fulfilled. The pastoral is not your genre, and Zuckerman Domesticus now seems to you just that, too easy a solution, an idyll of the kind you hate, a fantasy of innocence in the perfect house in the perfect landscape on the banks of the perfect stretch of river" (317). Roth's rejection of the pastoral, however, extends beyond personal matters or artistic sensibility, but finds its greatest resonance as Roth reconsiders American history in his fiction of the 1990s and early 2000s.

The dismantling of the pastoral myth or impulse remains most keenly felt, not surprisingly, in Roth's 1997 novel, *American Pastoral*. That novel's protagonist, Seymour "the Swede" Levov, a former high school baseball star and Marine turned glove factory owner, has his personal life and faith in American goodness ripped apart when his only daughter, Merry, bombs the local post office, an attack that kills an innocent doctor. As he considers how the bombing has radically reoriented the Swede's life, Nathan Zuckerman speculates that it's Merry "who transports [the Swede] out of the longed-for American pastoral and into everything that is its antithesis and its enemy, into the fury, the violence, and the desperation of the counterpastoral—into the indigenous American berserk" (86). Zuckerman's notion of the "indigenous American berserk" signals how, for Roth, the sense of social disarray embodied by the protests and the assassinations of the late 1960s is not so much a product of a particular historical moment, but a malevolent strain that has existed since the nation's founding that continuously asserts itself in our shared social, cultural, and political life. Roth's recognition of the "nearly demonic reality" of American life remains central to the chaotic notion of history that emerges in his fiction. "Madness and provocation. Nothing recognizable," Roth writes near the conclusion of the novel as the Swede comes to terms with how his teenage daughter's crime has reshaped his sense of reality. "No context in which it hangs together. *He* no longer hangs together. Even his capacity for suffering no longer exists" (371).[6]

The break that Zuckerman describes here—a fall from innocence that can never be healed—drives the sense of history that Roth pursues throughout the American Trilogy. The series counters the triumphalist narrative of the United States' postwar trajectory; in it, Roth dismantles the belief in progress that has so frequently colored the United States' sense of itself as a nation. What Roth would seem to be asking in these novels is: how do we make sense of our national history once the veil of innocence has been lifted? How do we continue once we have become estranged from our sense of ourselves and our nation? These are the unanswerable questions that Roth pursues throughout much of his fiction and that make his reading of American history particularly resonant in times of political and cultural crisis. Like many of his contemporaries (John Updike, Ralph Ellison, Norman Mailer, James Baldwin, Joan Didion, Thomas Pynchon, Toni Morrison), Roth captured the violence and fragmentation that characterized American life in the second half of the twentieth century, with a heightened awareness of how the myths of American exceptionalism, myths instilled in Roth as a child during the Great Depression and the Second World War, made that fragmentation feel more acutely painful.

What gives these questions resonance, however, is Roth's capacity to capture the details of a life lived in America. Roth's insistence on specificity—for example, the outrageous sexual exploits graphically depicted in *Portnoy's Complaint*; and the details of operating a butcher shop in *Indignation*—gives his fiction its impact and grounds the competing voices that inhabit his work in a visceral reality. The novel, for Roth, is not a means for resolving or simplifying our problems; instead, it is the vehicle that best captures life's fascinating and galling contradictions. "I am a theater and nothing more than a theater," Zuckerman proclaims at the conclusion of *The Counterlife*, the novel in which Roth most fully embraces postmodern indeterminacy (321). Zuckerman's assertion that he is "nothing more than a theater" also illustrates the centrality of performance—the freedom to try on new masks and novel positions—to Roth's fiction. To identify the real position of "Philip Roth" through his fiction, to untangle what Roth really believes—about himself, masculine desire, Jewish identity, Israel, America—is an impossible task. "Making fake biography, false history, concocting a half-imaginary existence out of the actual drama of my life *is* my life," Roth observed in his 1984 *Paris Review* interview with Hermione Lee. "There has to be some pleasure in this job, and that's it. To go around in disguise. To act a character. To pass oneself off as what one is not. To *pretend*" (*Why Write?* 146). The contradictory voices that populate his novels cannot be reduced, silenced, or amalgamated into a single authoritative perspective. For Roth, the novel is the best vehicle for rendering all that cannot be resolved within our lives, fiction getting us closer to reality than a straight recording of the facts ever could. In "The Ruthless Intimacy of Fiction" (2013), Roth observed, "This passion for specificity, for the hypnotic materiality of the world one is in, is all but at the heart of the task to which every American novelist has been enjoined since Herman Melville and his whale and Mark Twain and his river: to discover the most arresting, evocative verbal depiction for every last American thing" (*Why Write?* 393).

Shaped by the twin traumas of the Depression and the Second World War, Roth developed a certain critical patriotic attachment to his nation that belied a deeper love of America. "For [his daughter], being an American was loathing America, but loving America was something he could not let go of any more than he could have let go of loving his father and his mother, any more than he could have let go of his decency," Roth writes of Swede Levov's love of his nation in *American Pastoral*, a sentiment that reflects the affection that Roth also felt (213). Roth's connection to America would certainly be seriously challenged by the many political and social upheavals that occurred during his fifty-year career—he was an outspoken critic of Richard Nixon and the Vietnam War and later was a vocal opponent of both George W. Bush and Donald Trump—but it remained an integral part of Roth's understanding of himself as a writer. Moreover, while critics often identified Roth as a Jewish American writer, the heir to Bernard Malamud and Saul Bellow, he consistently rejected such labeling. Instead, he insisted that his work transcends the particularities of the Jewish experience in the United States, even if it is in some ways informed by them. "The Jewish quality of books like mine doesn't really reside in their subject matter," Roth noted in his *Paris Review* interview. "Talking about Jewishness hardly interests me at all. It's a kind of sensibility that makes, say, *The Anatomy Lesson* [1983] Jewish, if anything does: the nervousness, the excitability, the arguing, the dramatizing, the indignation, the obsessiveness, the touchiness, the play-acting—above all the *talking*. The talking and the shouting. Jews will go on, you know. It isn't what it's talking *about* that makes a book Jewish—it's that the book won't shut up" (*Why Write?* 161).

In his late-career essay "I Have Fallen in Love with American Names" (2002), Roth distances himself even more from the notion of the Jewish, or the Jewish American, novelist. In that essay, Roth acknowledges the American novelists (Theodore Dreiser, Sherwood Anderson, Ring Lardner, Sinclair Lewis, Thomas Wolfe, and Erskine Caldwell), "mainly small-town midwesterners and southerners," who inspired his literary ambitions as an adolescent and "who shaped and expanded my sense of America" (*Why Write?* 331–2). "Yes,

I had been born to these parents, in this time, with their struggles, but I would volunteer to become the child of these writers as well," Roth writes, "and through my immersion in their fiction try to apprehend their American places as a second reality that was, to an American kid in a Jewish neighborhood in industrial Newark, a vivifying expansion of his own" (*Why Write?* 332). At the conclusion of that essay, Roth remarks that his "generation of native born— whose omnipresent spectacle was the U.S.A.'s shifting fortunes in a prolonged global war against totalitarian evil and who came of age and matured, as high school and college students, during the remarkable makeover of the postwar decade and the alarming onset of the Cold War—for us no such self-limiting label could ever seem commensurate with our experience as Americans, with all that means, for good and ill" *(Why Write?* 335).

Roth's sense of himself as first and foremost an American was inevitably and profoundly informed by his Newark childhood in the middle decades of the twentieth century. Born March 19, 1933, at the depths of the Great Depression, Roth was the second son of Herman and Bess Roth (his older brother Sanford ["Sandy"] had been born in 1927). His parents were the children of immigrants: his father's family had emigrated from Polish Galicia, a region that straddles Poland and the Ukraine, while his mother's parents had originated in the Kiev region of Ukraine.[7] Herman Roth was an insurance broker with Metropolitan Life, and Bess was a devoted homemaker and mother to her two sons, and Roth grew up in a family whose closeness he perceived as characteristic of the Jewish families he was surrounded by growing up in Weequahic. Neither of Roth's parents were readers—as Roth notes in a 1969 essay in support of the Newark Public Library, his "family did not own many books, or have the money for a child to buy them" (*Reading Myself* 176)—but he was inspired by his beloved older brother's artistic ambitions (as an adult, Sandy worked in advertising before pursuing painting in retirement, a career trajectory that Roth would give the protagonist of his 2006 novel *Everyman*).[8] Writing in *The Facts*, Roth explains, "The link to my father was never so voluptuously tangible as the colossal bond to my mother's flesh, whose metamorphosed incarnation was a sleek black sealskin coat into which I, the younger, the privileged, the pampered papoose, blissfully wormed myself when my father chauffeured us home to New Jersey on a winter Sunday" (18).[9] Despite this affection, Roth's relationship to his mother was more "complicated"; biographer Blake Bailey says Roth occasionally "conceded that Sophie Portnoy [the overbearing Jewish mother in *Portnoy's Complaint*] was somewhat modeled on the more 'suffocating' mother his older brother had known as a little boy, when Bess was younger, poorer, and under a strain," and Roth's psychiatrist Hans Kleinschmidt in 1967 surmised that Roth's "main problem was castration anxiety vis-à-vis a phallic mother figure."[10]

While he remained sheltered by his mother's love, Roth's relationship with his father was more combative, though no less significant. Roth would movingly write of their relationship in his 1991 memoir *Patrimony: A True Story*, and Herman Roth can be felt in many of the overly emotional and protective fathers that populate Roth's fiction. "However awkward the union may sometimes have been," Roth writes of the relationship, "vulnerable to differences of opinion, to false, expectations, to radically divergent experiences of America, strained by the colliding of two impatient, equally willful temperaments and marred by masculine clumsiness, the link to him has been omnipresent" (*The Facts* 16). Despite the conflict, Roth remained deeply devoted to his father, the two firmly connected by both the love and the tensions that defined their relationship. "Narrative is the form that [my father's] knowledge takes," Roth acknowledges in *The Facts*, "and his repertoire has never been large: family, family, family, Newark, Newark, Newark, Jew, Jew, Jew. Somewhat like mine" (16). In *Patrimony*, Roth acknowledges how his father ultimately shaped his sense of what constitutes an American voice: "He *was* the vernacular, unpoetic and expressive and point-blank, with all the vernacular's glaring limitations and all its durable force" (181).

Although Roth frequently returned to Newark and the stories of his family that his father instilled in him, the time he spent in the city was relatively brief; his affection for the place was made possible by his sense that Newark was ultimately too provincial for his artistic and intellectual ambitions.[11] That said, the details that fuel so much of Roth's fiction come from his childhood in the Weequahic neighborhood of Newark where he spent his boyhood years. "Newark was a city filled with upward-striving immigrants—there were significant populations not only of Jews but of Italians, Irish, Germans, and African Americans up from the South—although each group maintained its own staked-out area," Claudia Roth Pierpont writes of the city in the opening decades of the twentieth century. "The Weequahic section, where the Roth family lived, was an almost wholly Jewish enclave in the southwest corner of the city. Fully developed only in the twenties and thirties, it was settled by first-generation American Jews eager to leave the crowded squalor of their parents' immigrant quarters in central Newark's Third Ward, where Herman Roth was born in 1901."[12] As he recalls the neighborhood in *The Facts*, Roth's attachment is plainly evident: "When the weather was good we'd sometimes wind up back of Chancellor Avenue School, on the wooden bleachers along the sidelines of the asphalt playground adjacent to the big dirt playing field. Stretched on our backs in the open night air, we were as carefree as any kids anywhere in postwar America, and we certainly felt ourselves no less American" (31). In a 2000 interview, Roth echoed this sentiment: "My experience had been about our aggression, our going out into Newark, three or four of us, wandering the streets at night, shooting crap in back of the high school with flashlights, girls, going after your date to this gathering place called Syd's on Chancellor Avenue and telling your sex stories. It was that verbal robustness, people talking, being terrifically funny, playing ball, competing, the energy flowing out. . . . Appetite. Maybe that's the word. It was the appetites that were aggressive."[13]

Indeed, Roth's memories of Newark remain the most consistent element that runs throughout his fiction; it seems perfectly fitting, then, that he would bookend his career with two books, *Goodbye, Columbus* and *Nemesis*, set in Newark. "Sitting there in the park, I felt a deep knowledge of Newark," Neil Klugman affirms early in *Goodbye, Columbus*, "an attachment so rooted that it could not help but branch out into affection" (31). The fondness that the young Klugman, who is only three years removed from college in the novella, feels for his hometown would grow more complicated, more painful, as Roth's male protagonists aged, especially in the wake of the 1967 riots that transformed Newark's cityscape and permanently altered its political, economic, and social trajectory. As historian Rick Perlstein notes, by the year of the riots "Newark had the highest percentage of substandard housing of any American city: 7,097 units had no flush toilets; 28,795, no heaters. Twenty-eight babies died in a diarrhea epidemic in 1965, eighteen of them at City Hospital, which was also infested by bats. The city's major industry was illegal gambling. Cops ran heroin rings. Food stores raised prices the day welfare checks arrived. All the same, downtown was filled with construction cranes. 'Urban renewal' served Mayor [Hugh] Addonizio's political purpose: by continually scattering Negroes, who were 65 percent of the population, it radically reduced their power."[14] The riots would irrevocably alter Roth's sense of his hometown; their impact is central to *American Pastoral*'s depiction of the upheaval of the late 1960s. "There were no longer stories of old," Roth writes of Newark in the aftermath of the riots in that novel. "There was nothing. There was a mattress, discolored and waterlogged, like a cartoon-strip drunk slumped against a pole. The pole still held up a sign telling you what corner you were on. And that's all there was" (236).

Perhaps not surprisingly, Roth would repeatedly return in his fiction to the vanquished world of his childhood; while never a sentimental or nostalgic writer, Roth would cast Newark's fate as a sort of tragedy that reflected the crumbling of the United States' post-1945 political and cultural expansion, his later work relishing conserving his sense of a place that had been radically transformed during his lifetime. It is fitting that Zuckerman's forty-fifth high school reunion in *American Pastoral* does not take place in Newark, but in a suburban country club, a setting that reinforces the sense that the Newark of Zuckerman's youth no longer exists, heightening the loneliness and sense of loss that drives his subsequent reimagining of Seymour Levov's life in the novel. "Am I wrong to think that we delighted in living there? No delusions are more familiar than those inspired in the elderly by nostalgia, but am I completely mistaken to think that living as well-born children in Renaissance Florence could not have held a candle to growing up within aromatic range of Tabachnik's pickle barrels? Am I mistaken to think that even back then, in the vivid present, the fullness of life stirred our emotions to an extraordinary extent," Zuckerman asks in *American Pastoral*, suggesting that the vanquished Newark grew in importance for Roth in the decades after the 1967 riots. "Has anywhere since so engrossed you in its ocean of details? The *detail*, the immensity of the detail, the force of the detail, the weight of the detail—the rich endlessness of detail surrounding you in your young life like the six feet of dirt that'll be packed on your grave when you're dead" (42–3).

Despite his later professed connection to Newark, Roth left the city behind after completing his freshman year of college at Newark College of Rutgers when he decided to transfer to Bucknell University, a small liberal arts college located in Lewisburg, Pennsylvania.[15] Roth's decision to attend Bucknell reflected his larger fascination with making his way into the America that existed outside of the confines of Newark, a notion that would propel his first two novels, *Letting Go* and *When She Was Good*. "To be sure, everything about the rural landscape and the small-town setting . . . suggested an unmistakably gentile version of unpretentious civility," Roth recalls of Bucknell in *The Facts*, "but by 1951 none of us thought it pretentious or unseemly that the momentum of our family's Americanization should have carried us, in half a century, from my Yiddish-speaking grandparents' hard existence in Newark's poorest ghetto neighborhood to this pretty place whose harmonious nativeness was proclaimed in every view" (46). In a 1981 interview, he elaborated on his motivations for choosing to attend college in rural Pennsylvania: "So I chose an ordinary college in a pretty little town in a beautiful farming valley in central Pennsylvania about which I knew practically nothing, where I went to chapel once a week with the Christian boys and girls who were my classmates, youngsters from conventional backgrounds with predominately philistine interests. My attempt to throw myself whole-heartedly into the traditional college life of that era [the early 1950s] lasted about six months, though chapel I could never stomach and I made it a habit conspicuously to be reading Schopenhauer in my pew during the sermon" (*Why Write?* 129).

At Bucknell, Roth's interest in literature and writing would blossom; in his junior year, he would become editor-in-chief of the school's satirical newspaper, *Et Cetra*, demonstrating a talent for satire and humor that he would fully embrace in *Portnoy's Complaint* (*The Facts* 62). While Roth bristled at the conventions that defined the social world of Bucknell—an experience that he would recall in *The Facts* and fictionalize in *Indignation*—he excelled at the school, graduating *magna cum laude* in English and elected to Phi Beta Kappa. While recounting in *The Facts* why he pledged with the Jewish fraternity over "a nominally Christian but essentially areligious fraternity," Roth explains that he came to accept what he describes as "the exuberant side of my personality, the street-corner taste for comic mockery and for ludicrous, theatrical speculation" (50, 51). It was an aspect of his personality that he saw as a product of his Jewish upbring in Newark and that he perceived as essential to his particular performance of American identity. "I wasn't afraid of the temptation to become an honorary WASP," Roth says of his fraternity decision in *The Facts*, "but was leery of a communal spirit that might lead to self-censorship, since the last thing I'd left home for was to become encased in somebody else's idea of what I should be" (51).

After graduating from Bucknell in 1954, Roth accepted a scholarship to the University of Chicago, where he completed his Master's in English literature in 1955. Later that year, he enlisted in the US Army but received an honorable discharge in 1956 after sustaining a back injury.[16] After his discharge, Roth returned to the University of Chicago, where he started the Ph.D. program in English literature; he left the graduate program after one semester but stayed on at the university to teach in the composition program. While at Chicago, Roth befriended Saul Bellow, (they would remain friends until Bellow's death in 2005) and began working on the stories that would later become his first book, *Goodbye, Columbus*. In 1958, two of Roth's short stories, "The Conversion of the Jews" and "Epstein," appeared in *The Paris Review*, and in 1959 he released *Goodbye, Columbus* (which includes the title novella and five other stories including the two that had been published in *The Paris Review*). The collection would go on to win the National Book Award, the first of two that Roth would win. Despite the accolades that *Goodbye, Columbus* generated, Roth also received a barrage of criticism from the Jewish American establishment, many of whom felt his depiction of Jewish life would provide fodder for anti-Semitism. Perhaps most notably, Roth came under attack in 1962 while participating in a symposium with Ralph Ellison at Yeshiva University in New York City, an experience that Roth revisited in the essay "Writing about Jews" (1963). "My humiliation before the Yeshiva belligerents—indeed, the angry

Jewish resistance that I aroused virtually from the start," Roth later recalled in *The Facts*, "was the luckiest break I could have had. I was branded" (130).

During his tenure in Chicago, Roth also met Margaret ("Maggie") Martinson Williams, a divorced mother of two who had grown up in an abusive home, whom he married in 1959. Much the way Roth's decision to attend Bucknell was inspired by his desire to discover the "real" America, his relationship with Williams was shaped by his fascination with how she appeared to embody the rough-edged gentile America chronicled in Dreiser's fiction, an existence that Roth longed to experience. "I was, to the contrary, thrilled by this opportunity to distinguish at first hand between American realities and shtetl legend," Roth writes in *The Facts*, "to surmount the instinctive repugnance of my clan to prove myself superior to folk superstitions that enlightened, democratic spirits like me no longer had dignified need of in the heterogenous U.S.A. And to prove myself superior as well to Jewish trepidation by dint of taming the most fearsome female that a boy of my background might be unfortunate enough to meet on the erotic battlefield" (84). The marriage itself would prove to be disastrous—the relationship would become fodder for many of his early novels, including *Letting Go*, *When She Was Good*, and most explicitly in *My Life as a Man*, which Roth jokingly described in his 1984 *Paris Review* interview as "the war novel I wrote some years after failing to receive the Distinguished Service Cross" (*Why Write?* 150). They would separate in 1962, but their marriage would not legally end until Williams died in a car accident in 1968. "Without doubt she was my worst enemy ever," Roth remarked in *The Facts*, "but, alas, she was also nothing less than the greatest creative-writing teacher of them all, specialist par excellence in the aesthetics of extremist fiction" (112). In *The Facts*, Roth claims that Maggie, whom he calls "Josie" in the memoir, faked a pregnancy—and later an abortion—so that Roth would marry her, an episode that he inserted directly into *My Life as a Man* and that revealed to him the potential of reality to be "more interesting" and more extreme than even the most outlandish fiction that he could concoct (107).

A year after the success of *Goodbye, Columbus,* Roth accepted a visiting lectureship at the University of Iowa's Writers' Workshop, and two years later he became writer-in-residence at Princeton University. He would go on in 1965 to join the faculty of the University of Pennsylvania, where he would intermittently teach comparative literature for about a decade. In 1962, he published his first full-length novel *Letting Go*, a work heavily indebted to Henry James that focuses on the moral crises facing two English literature graduate students and their romantic partners. Five years later, he released *When She Was Good*, a relatively minor novel featuring Roth's only female protagonist; its release

did little to help bolster his critical or popular standing. It was the publication of the sexually explicit *Portnoy's Complaint* at the end of the 1960s that
catapulted Roth into the literary stratosphere, making him for a time both a
literary celebrity and a figure of notoriety. Taking the form of a psychoanalytic
monologue—the novel consists of Alex Portnoy's attempt to account for his
sexual life and family history to his analyst, Dr. Otto Spielvogel (who remains
silent except for the novel's famous last line, "Now vee may perhaps to begin.
Yes?")—*Portnoy's Complaint* would become something of a cultural phenomenon (274). Roth's explicit and frequently hilarious depiction of Alex Portnoy's
sexual exploits, especially his adventures in masturbation, would seem to be a
product, or perhaps a reflection, of the Sexual Revolution. Beyond the novel's
cultural import, the book also signaled a breakthrough for Roth as he shed the
narrative constraints, the moral seriousness, that he had inherited from James
and Chekhov, to create a new sort of freewheeling narrative.

In the wake of *Portnoy*'s tremendous success, Roth went on to write a series of comedic novels—*Our Gang* (1971), *The Breast* (1972), and *The Great
American Novel*—that continued the unrestrained narrative approach that had
characterized *Portnoy's Complaint*. In 1973, he became the General Editor of
Penguin's "Writers from the Other Europe" series, which introduced writers
such as Milan Kundera, Bruno Schulz, Ivan Klíma, and Danilo Kis to American readers. During this period, Roth regularly travelled to Prague where he
met with such writers as Klíma, Miroslav Holub, and Karel Sidon; he would
also befriend Milan Kundera, who had emigrated to France in 1975. Perhaps
not surprisingly, this experience in Eastern Europe would bleed into Roth's
own work, most notably *The Professor of Desire* (1977) and *The Prague Orgy*
(1985).[17] Observing his advocacy for Eastern European writers, Ira Nadel contends that Roth "transformed" in the 1970s and '80s into America's most Eu-
rocentric, politically conscious writer, anticipating his later engagement with
America's social and political problems" in his later work.[18] In 1975, he moved
to London with the actress Claire Bloom and began dividing his time between
the UK and his home in Connecticut. The relationship with Bloom would last
for more than a decade; they would marry in 1990 but separate three years later.
Bloom published a memoir, *Leaving a Doll's House* (1996), that chronicled the
deterioration of their relationship and depicted Roth in a less-than-flattering
light; Roth would subsequently consider Bloom's book to be "among the worst
catastrophes of his life and credited [it] with his failure to win the Nobel."[19]

Toward the end of the 1970s, Roth returned to the character of Nathan
Zuckerman, a character first introduced as one of Peter Tarnopol's fictional
creations in *My Life as a Man*, in the Zuckerman Bound series—*The Ghost
Writer* (1979), *Zuckerman Unbound* (1981), *The Anatomy Lesson*, and *The*

Prague Orgy. These novels trace the life and career of a Jewish American writer whose trajectory closely follows the contours of Roth's biography; in his glowing review of the novels, Harold Bloom described them as "the bleakest and the funniest writing Roth has done" and argued that the series should be read as "a classic apologia, an aggressive defense of Roth's moral stance as an author."[20] Beyond just offering a defense of Roth's creative approach, the Zuckerman novels rigorously explore the ethical implications of the writing life. In the early books of the series, Roth explores how Zuckerman's professional life irreparably damages his relationship with his family, his father calling him "a bastard" on his deathbed (*Zuckerman Unbound* 193). "You *are* a bastard," Henry screams at his older brother in the concluding section of *Zuckerman Unbound*. "A heartless conscienceless bastard. What does loyalty mean to you? What does responsibility mean to you? What does self-denial mean, *restraint*—anything at all? To you everything is disposable! Everything is *ex*posable! Jewish morality, Jewish endurance, Jewish wisdom, Jewish families—everything is grist for your fun-machine" (217).

Zuckerman's proclivity for transgression—scandalizing his family and betraying the trust of his friends and lovers—remains crucial to his sense of his literary identity, one deeply informed by the almost religious belief in the import of art and literature that he (and Roth) had internalized during their college and graduate education. Ross Posnock usefully observes, "Roth's own assault on purity can't escape the inflated selfhood of the alienated intellectual, a posture that is symptomatic of the American reflex to heroicize, hence to simplify and purify."[21] The same diagnosis applies to Zuckerman, who in his youth embraces his transgressions and his alienation as vital to his attempts to define himself as an individual and as an artist. Zuckerman identifies, and at times embraces, the desire to break free from all the constraints (familial, communal, religious, ethnic) that can thwart a radical course of self-determination. At the same time, he recognizes the costs, the irreparable damage, such acts of radical self-definition often engender. Suffering writer's block and tremendous physical pain in the wake of his father's death in *The Anatomy Lesson*, Zuckerman describes how "memories of his father's last years, of the strain between them, the bitterness, the bewildering estrangement, gnawed away at him along with [his brother] Henry's dubious accusation; so did the curse his father had fastened with his dying breath; so did the idea that he written what he had, as he had, simply to be odious, that his work embodied little more than stubborn defiance toward a respectable chiropodist" (40).

Throughout the Zuckerman novels, Roth also expands Nathan's story, enabling it to reflect the shifting status of American literary culture from the 1950s ethos that emboldened the aspiring novelist to the more anemic and fragmented one he encounters as an older writer in *Exit Ghost*. *The Ghost Writer* depicts a young Zuckerman, flush off the success of publishing his first short stories that chronicle the foibles of contemporary Jewish American life, enamored with the promises of the literary life. E. I. Lonoff, the older author whom the younger Nathan idolizes in the novel, attempts to disabuse the younger writer of his romantic notions of being a professional writer. "I turn sentences around. That's my life," Lonoff warns Zuckerman at the beginning of the book. "I write a sentence and then I turn it around. Then I look at it and I turn it around again. Then I have lunch. Then I come back in and write another sentence. Then I have tea and turn the new sentence around. Then I read the two sentences over and turn them both around. Then I lie down on my sofa and think. Then I get up and throw them out and start from the beginning. And if I knock off from this routine for as long as a day, I'm frantic with boredom and a sense of waste" (17–8). Lonoff's creative process would seem to reflect Roth's own approach, suggesting the tediousness and loneliness (and even physicality) that a sustained career as an author demands. "50 years in a room silent as the bottom of a pool, eking out, when all went well, my minimum daily allowance of usable prose," Roth commented in one of his final interviews when asked about his memories of his professional career.[22]

While the Zuckerman Bound sequence was relatively well-received by critics, the publication of the postmodern-inflected *The Counterlife* in 1986, in retrospect, truly inaugurated the second half of Roth's career. At the same time as he was enjoying renewed critical appreciation, Roth experienced a series of health crises that nearly derailed his career and his life. Throughout the mid-1980s, he suffered from near-debilitating back pain, then a knee injury suffered while swimming resulted in surgery, and after that surgery he was prescribed the sleeping aid Halcion, which caused him to fall into a suicidal depression. "My mind began to disintegrate," the fictional Philip Roth says of his experience with Halcion in *Operation Shylock*. "The word DISINTEGRATION seemed itself to be the matter out of which my brain was constituted and it began spontaneously coming apart" (20). Finally, at the end of the decade Roth "underwent emergency quintuple bypass surgery, the same dangerous procedure that he had given to both Zuckerman brothers in *The Counterlife*."[23]

In the immediate aftermath of these crises, Roth would go on to enjoy his most successful decade as an author, a rather remarkable feat for a writer in his sixties. After partially setting *The Counterlife* and *Operation Shylock* in Israel and exploring complex issues such as Zionism and the aftermath of the Holocaust, Roth brought his fiction back home in *Sabbath's Theater*, a book that propelled the exploration of American history that would define the American

Trilogy. In a 2000 interview, Roth explained what inspired him to return to the American scene in his fiction after a prolonged period of alternating between London and Connecticut:

> When I look back now, I see that *Sabbath's Theater* is the real turning back to American stuff. Mickey Sabbath's is such an American voice. And after him, if not out of him, came the American trilogy. And I see from what I'm writing right now that even if I try, I can't steer clear of our common history creeping thematically into my work. This is a result of growing older, I suppose. You don't have a historical perspective for a long time. A historical perspective requires time. Then, alas, time passes, you've got one and you're stuck with it.[24]

This sense of a "historical perspective" distinguishes and elevates much of Roth's later fiction as he and his characters attempt to comprehend the history that has shaped their sense of themselves and their nation. Returning to the character of Nathan Zuckerman, Roth employed his long-standing alter-ego to contemplate the United States' post-1945 experience.[25] Vis-à-vis Zuckerman, Roth considers his generation's unique perspective on the political and cultural upheavals that transformed the US in the post-1945 era. "The generation known in its college years as 'silent,'" Roth wrote in a 1974 self-interview, "was in actuality straitjacketed, at its most dismal bound by the pieties, fantasies, and values that one might expect to hear articulated today only by a genuine oddball like Tricia Nixon" (*Reading Myself* 88).

In many ways, the American Trilogy reflects the myths, "the pieties" and "fantasies," that Roth's generation had to shed as they experienced the upheavals of the 1960s that upended the more benevolent version of their nation they had absorbed as children. Alongside novels such as Toni Morrison's *Paradise* (1998), Norman Mailer's *Harlot's Ghost* (1991), Thomas Pynchon's *Mason & Dixon* (1997), John Updike's *In the Beauty of the Lilies* (1996), Joan Didion's *The Last Thing He Wanted* (1996), and Don DeLillo's *Underworld* (1997), all works published in the 1990s, the American Trilogy endeavored to come to terms with the history of the United States as it emerged from the shadow of the Cold War. The trilogy would also initiate for Roth a new way of writing about history. Derek Parker Royal argues that "all three novels show how individual identity embodies *national* identity and how the forces of history—American history, specifically—threaten to overtake personal freedom and individual agency."[26] While the series revisits the ideas and arguments that Roth pursued in *Goodbye, Columbus* and *Portnoy's Complaint*, there is a heightened awareness in these later books of how the larger events of history infiltrate and alter our sense of ourselves. History, as it manifests itself in the American Trilogy, is a relentless and unknowable force that utterly transforms and disorients the individual.

In subsequent works, Roth moved from the cultural and political questions that swept the nation in the decades after the Second World War to considering the broader problem of history—of how the scholarly study of the past disguises what Roth terms in his counterfactual *The Plot Against America* as "the relentless unforeseen" (113–4). The novel, a counterhistory where Charles Lindbergh defeats Franklin Delano Roosevelt in the 1940 Presidential election and subsequently signs a non-aggression treaty with Nazi Germany, would become Roth's biggest commercial success since *Portnoy's Complaint* and would win the James Fenimore Cooper Prize for Best Historical Fiction. The notion of "the relentless unforeseen" that propels *The Plot Against America* would be central to Roth's late work: the final Nathan Zuckerman novel, *Exit Ghost,* and the four brief books that constitute the Nemeses tetralogy *(Everyman, Indignation, The Humbling* [2009], and *Nemesis).* Throughout the Nemeses series, Roth explores how uncontrolled forces can derail a life. In 2012, two years after the publication of *Nemesis,* Roth announced his retirement from fiction in an interview with the French magazine *Les Inrockuptibles.* Explaining his decision, Roth described how after completing *Nemesis* he reread all his work to see if he had "wasted my time" and concluded that he was content to step away from writing.[27] In the years after announcing his retirement, Roth remained active, but nevertheless maintained a very low public profile. In retirement, he largely avoided making appearances—he declared a 2014 reading at the 92nd Street Y in Manhattan to be his final public reading[28]—and with a few notable exceptions he eschewed giving interviews. In his final years, Roth devoted a great deal of energy to helping organize material for his official biographer, Blake Bailey, and oversaw the publication of *Why Write: Collected Nonfiction 1960–2013* (2017), the final volume in the Library of America's collection of his work.[29] Roth died from congestive heart failure in May 2018. Three years later, Bailey's authorized biography, simply entitled *Philip Roth: The Biography* (2021), was published by W.W. Norton & Company. However, allegations of sexual assault against Bailey quickly led Norton to take the book out of distribution (Skyhorse Publishing then secured rights to the book and released paperback, audiobook, and e-book editions in the United States).[30] The accusations against Bailey severely altered the reception of the biography and renewed critical discussions regarding Roth's treatment of women and sex in his fiction.[31]

In the years after his death, Roth's cultural prominence expanded as *The Plot Against America* seemed to anticipate the political crises triggered by

Donald Trump's presidency. Indeed, many cultural critics cited the novel, in which Lindbergh appeals to nativist (and anti-Semitic) sentiment to win the presidency, as being a central text for understanding Trump's political rise. Delivering the third annual Philip Roth Lecture in 2018, Salman Rushdie opined that Roth at the end of his career "ended up as a kind of prophet, a Cassandra for our age, warning us what was to come, and, like Cassandra, not being taken seriously."[32] Rushdie's reading of Roth's relevance in today's divisive political environment is noteworthy, suggesting how novels like *The Plot Against America* and *American Pastoral* capture the uncertainty that has always shaped the American experience. Perhaps not surprisingly, David Simon and Ed Burns positioned their televised adaptation of *The Plot Against America*, which premiered as a miniseries on HBO in 2020, as an explicit rebuke of the xenophobia and destruction of democratic norms that the Trump presidency occasioned.

Although his later novels have gained special resonance in recent years—his final novel *Nemesis* imagines a fictional polio outbreak in Newark in 1944 that reverberates with the panic that the COVID-19 pandemic triggered in 2020—Roth's thirty-one books offer a fascinating reflection of his nation during his lifetime. "History had been scaled down and personalized, America had been scaled down and personalized," Zuckerman observes in *I Married a Communist*, the second installment of the American Trilogy; "for me, that was the enchantment not only of [the playwright] Norman Corwin but of the times. You flood into history and history floods into you. You flood into America and America floods into you" (39). Indeed, Zuckerman's notion of how "America floods into you" succinctly encapsulates how Roth conceptualized himself as a novelist and a citizen. In one of his final interviews, Roth summed up his career as "exhilaration and groaning. Frustration and freedom. Inspiration and uncertainty. Abundance and emptiness. Blazing forth and muddling through."[33] The contradictions of the writer's existence remain central to much of his fiction, but by transforming his experience into fictional narrative, by remaining so devoted to his craft for over fifty years, Roth ultimately constructed one of the richest bodies of work in American letters, one that reveals the darkly hilarious and often maddening experience of having been alive for the better part of the "American century" as the United States struggled to maintain its benevolent self-image in the face of the destructive forces born of its particular history and national consciousness.

CHAPTER 2

Early Works

From *Goodbye, Columbus* to *My Life as a Man*

Recalling the opening decade of his career in a 1973 self-interview, Philip Roth observed he had once "imagined fiction to be something like a religious calling, and literature a kind of sacrament, a sense of things I have had reason to modify since. Such elevated notions aren't (or weren't, back then) that uncommon in vain young writers; they dovetailed nicely in my case with a penchant for ethical striving that I had absorbed as a Jewish child, and with the salvationist literary ethos in which I had been introduced to high art in the fifties, a decade when cultural, rather than political, loyalties divided the young into the armies of the damned and the cadre of the blessed." (*Reading Myself* 77–8). Roth's comments reflect the moral seriousness that defines his first three books, *Goodbye, Columbus and Five Short Stories* (1959), *Letting Go* (1962), and *When She Was Good* (1967), a propriety that Roth had inherited from his literary education as an English major during the early 1950s. As Morris Dickstein notes, Roth was certainly not alone in his assumption regarding fiction's spiritual value and function in an increasingly secular and commercial culture—that notion can be felt throughout much of the work of his contemporaries, a generation that included Ralph Ellison, John Updike, Susan Sontag, Toni Morrison, Thomas Pynchon, James Baldwin, Joan Didion, Norman Mailer, and Don DeLillo, to name but a few.

This chapter will focus on the opening phase of Roth's career—the fifteen-year period spanning *Goodbye, Columbus* to *My Life as a Man* (1974). Roth's reaction to the political and cultural upheaval of those fifteen years can be felt as he transformed himself from the more restrained writer of *Goodbye, Columbus* and *Letting Go*, books very much informed by the literary education he had pursued as an undergraduate at Bucknell and as a graduate student at the University of Chicago, to the more outlandish writer of *Portnoy's Complaint* (1969) and *Our Gang* (1971), products of a writer who had little interest in censoring himself. Embracing his proclivity for comedy and rage, Roth's fiction during this span would seem to mirror the trajectory of the United States, as the nation moved from the conservatism of Eisenhower's America to the malaise and cynicism that afflicted the nation in the wake of the violence of the late 1960s. "The Vietnam War years were the most 'politicized' of my life," Roth recalled in a 1974 interview, suggesting how his seemingly apolitical fiction was shaped by the events of those years. "I spent my days during this war writing fiction, none of which on the face of it would appear to connect to politics. But by being 'politicized' I mean something other than writing about politics or even taking direct political action. I mean something akin to what ordinary citizens experience in countries like Czechoslovakia or Chile: a daily awareness of government *as a coercive force,* its continuous presence in one's thoughts as far more than just an institutionalized system of regulations and controls" (*Why Write?* 110). Moreover, the turbulence Roth experienced during this period—the charges of Jewish self-hatred that were leveled against him in the aftermath of *Goodbye, Columbus*; his troubled first marriage to Margaret Martinson Williams; his experience with psychoanalysis—can be felt in the development of his fiction as he liberated himself from the literary masters (James, Flaubert, Dreiser, Wolfe) who had shaped his earliest work to emerge as one of the most singular and provocative literary voices of his generation.

The mixture of seriousness and comedy that characterizes Roth's early fiction can be felt in his debut collection, *Goodbye, Columbus and Five Short Stories*. Published in May of 1959, *Goodbye, Columbus* immediately established Roth as one of the prominent writers of his generation. The collection would win the National Book Award in 1960, a victory that secured Roth's position as a rising literary voice, and the book's reception would inform his sense of himself as a writer for the first decade of his career. As Claudia Roth Pierpont observes, the book "received substantial praise from the 'four tigers of American Jewish literature,' as Roth identifie[d] Saul Bellow, Alfred Kazin, Irving Howe, and Leslie Fielder, all of whom recognized a strong voice and a fresh perspective—the next development in the saga of Jews in America to which they themselves belonged."[1] Taken together, the pieces collected in *Goodbye, Columbus* offer a finely wrought and ambivalent portrait of postwar Jewish American life, capturing the historical moment when many Jews would seem to be enjoying the social and economic security that the United States had secured in the wake of the Second World War. In her reading of Roth's early fiction, Victoria Aarons argues that the stories "collectively reveal a deeply felt ambivalence toward what it means to be Jewish in post–World War II America."[2] Of the book's reception, David Gooblar observes, "The Jewish response to *Goodbye, Columbus* had two distinct strains. The New York Intellectuals [Fielder, Howe, Kazin] praised Roth's cutting portrayal of the prosperous Jewish suburbs, affirming a modernist view of the artist who must maintain a critical eye toward his or her community. The outraged readers, by contrast, were precisely concerned with protecting that community, especially in regard to how it was seen by outsiders."[3]

Indeed, the Jews depicted in *Goodbye, Columbus* have mostly left the economic and cultural constraints that many first-generation immigrants experienced and have entered what they perceive as the mainstream of middle-class American life, moving from wholly urban Jewish enclaves into the newly formed suburbs. It is a trajectory best captured by the wealthy Brenda Patimkin, the object of Neil Klugman's desire, in the titular novella. Brenda's father owns a successful business, Patimkin Kitchen and Bathroom Sinks, and the family has left the urban confines of Newark's Third Ward for the wealth and suburban comfort of Short Hills, New Jersey. "It was, in fact, as though the hundred and eighty feet that the suburbs rose in altitude above Newark brought one closer to heaven," Neil Klugman observes as he drives to Short Hills to visit Brenda at the beginning of "Goodbye, Columbus," "for the sun itself became bigger, lower, and rounder, and soon I was driving past long lawns which seemed to be twirling water on themselves, and past houses where no one sat on stoops, where lights were on but no windows open, for those inside, refusing to share the very texture of life with those of us outside, regulated with a dial the amounts of moisture that were allowed access to their skin" (8–9). Later in the novella, Neil comments on how the Patimkin business was "in the heart of the Negro section of Newark" (90). Reflecting on the changes that had transformed the city, Neil muses, "The neighborhood had changed: the old Jews like my grandparents had struggled and died, and their offspring had struggled and prospered, and moved further and further west, towards the edge of Newark, then out of it, and up the slope of the Orange Mountains, until they had reached the crest and started down the other side, pouring into Gentile territory as the Scotch-Irish had poured through the Cumberland Gap" (90).

Such keen observations permeate the novella as Neil navigates the upper-middle-class milieu the Patimkins now inhabit. At twenty-three, a recent graduate of Newark Colleges of Rutgers and still living with his overbearing Aunt Gladys and Uncle Max, Neil is very much an outsider to the affluence that the Radcliffe-attending Brenda embodies. His character establishes the prototype for many of Roth's subsequent male protagonists: he is intelligent and observant, pulled by his sexual desire, but determined not to be constrained by what he sees as the confines of traditional family life. Neil, however, lacks the over-whelming ambition that drives most of Roth's later alter-egos—while he has graduated from college, he has no real ambitions beyond his current position at the Newark Public Library, telling Brenda that he hasn't "planned a thing in three years" (51). The novella chronicles Neil and Brenda's summer romance, tracing Neil's increased ambivalence toward what he sees as the emptiness of the Patimkins's upper-middle-class lifestyle, an ambivalence that ultimately dooms their relationship.

The affluence that characterizes the Patimkins's lifestyle—and the gap between their world in Short Hills and Neil's existence in Newark—is best captured in a scene where Neil marvels at all the fresh fruit stored in their basement refrigerator: "No longer did it hold butter, eggs, herring in cream sauce, ginger ale, tuna fish, an occasional corsage—rather it was heaped with fruit, shelves swelled with it, every color, every texture, and hidden within, every kind of pit. There were greenage plums, black plums, red plums, apricots, nectarines, peaches, long horns of grapes, black, yellow, red, and cherries, cherries flowing out of boxes and staining everything scarlet. And there were melons—cantaloupes and honeydews—and on the top shelf, half of a huge watermelon, a thin sheet of wax paper clinging to its bare red face like a wet lip. Oh Patimkin! Fruit grew in their refrigerator and sporting goods dropped from their trees!" (43). The seemingly endless supply of fresh fruit stands in stark contrast to the more austere food that his Aunt Gladys serves; she would never buy so much fruit in fear that it would go bad. Despite his skewering of the Patimkins's hidden fruit, Neil certainly enjoys the comforts of their home. In the following scene, he and Brenda make love for the first time, Roth aligning Neil's relishing of the fruit, notably the "handful" of overflowing cherries he grabs, with his sexual satisfaction (45, 43). The Patimkins would seem to embody a new form of Jewish American life, an upper-middle-class world of country clubs and affluence from which Jews had traditionally been excluded. Neil, however, remains uncertain about the life that a future with Brenda would entail. "Money and comfort would not erase [Brenda's] singleness—they hadn't yet, or had they," Neil muses midway through the novella as Brenda tries on various expensive dresses for her brother's pending nuptials. "What was I loving, I wondered, and since I am not one to stick scalpels into myself, I wiggled my hand in the fence and allowed a tiny-nosed buck to lick my thoughts away" (96).

Beyond its critique of privileged Jewish American life, "Goodbye, Columbus" features Roth's first foray into chronicling the tumult of male sexual desire, a facet of the male psyche that he would repeatedly explore in his later work. Written before the onset of the Sexual Revolution, the novella captures the difficulties facing young couples who wanted to engage in premarital sex in the years before the advent of the birth control pill, released in 1960, and before *Roe v. Wade*, which legalized abortion in 1973. Indeed, the plot centers on Neil's request that Brenda get a diaphragm, a request that she initially angrily resists. Despite his belief that he is the more enlightened of the two, Neil is ultimately a product of his culture as he badgers Brenda about their sexual behavior. Reflecting on his 1950s sexual education in *The Dying Animal* (2001), David Kepesh recalls how, in his young adulthood, "One was a thief in the sexual realm. You 'copped' a feel. You stole sex. You cajoled, you begged, you flattered, you insisted—all sex had to be struggled for, against the values if not the will of the girl" (66). Neil and Brenda would seem to be very much a product of the sexual climate that Kepesh later recounts. Describing their first sexual encounter, Neil notes that when he "began to unbutton [Brenda's] dress she resisted me, and I like to think it was because she knew how lovely she looked in it" (45). Neil's views of sex and of his relationship with Brenda remain deeply informed by the sexual conservatism of the 1950s; in hindsight, it is ultimately Brenda, whom Neil believes to be too conventional and myopic, who emerges as the more rebellious and interesting character as she pursues her relationship with Neil.

While "Goodbye, Columbus" captured the cultural and sexual ambiguities of contemporary Jewish American life, reflecting the uncertainties of a generation coming of age in a new era of American prosperity, the other stories in the collection triggered a much stronger reaction. In "The Conversion of the Jews," the collection's most overtly comic story, Ozzie Freedman, a boy of thirteen, runs to the roof of his synagogue and demands that his mother, his Hebrew teacher, and everyone watching from the ground below confess on bended knee that "they believed in Jesus Christ," after Ozzie has questioned the Hebrew teacher, Rabbi Binder, on whether God could have created a son without engaging in sexual intercourse with a woman (158). The story captures the hypocrisies of organized religion as Ozzie pesters the rabbi with questions that challenge the conventions of the faith; the story's wry critique of the adult world's unwillingness to respond to the boy's intellectual curiosity reflects a larger distrust of groups and institutions. It is a skepticism that seems very much in line with the larger cultural moment, the fear of conformity evident in works such as J. D. Salinger's *The Catcher in the Rye* (1951), Joseph Heller's *Catch-22* (1961), Ralph Ellison's *Invisible Man* (1952), and Sloan Wilson's *The Man in the Gray Flannel Suit* (1956).

Roth pursues questions regarding the Jewish faith and identity from a more serious perspective in the collection's other pieces. Three stories in particular—"Epstein," "Eli the Fanatic," and "Defender of the Faith"— triggered an outraged response from many Jewish American religious leaders, a critical blowback that the young Roth had not anticipated. In "Epstein," Roth follows an adulterous middle-aged Jewish man who suffers from a series of physical ailments resulting from his adulterous actions. "Eli, the Fanatic" covers more sensitive ground following Eli Peck, a lawyer, who is hired by his neighbors to remove a new Orthodox Yeshiva that houses eighteen refugee children within their suburban community because it disrupts the community's assimilated image. "You want to know something about those people, they're religious fanatics is what they are," one of Eli's inflamed neighbors tells the beleaguered lawyer. "Dressing like that. What goes on up there, Eli? That's what I'd really like to find out. I'm skeptical, Eli, I'm goddam skeptical" (276). The story's irony, of course, lies in how the Jews who have secured their position within suburban Christian America now feverishly work to exclude other Jews whom they fear will somehow endanger the social capital and acceptance they feel they have earned.

However, it was "Defender of the Faith" that generated the most controversy. The story's publication in the *New Yorker* was a major coup for the young Roth as it expanded his readership, putting him in the first rank of American fiction writers alongside the likes of J. D. Salinger and John Cheever. The story's publication in such a prominent magazine also inflamed many Jewish American religious leaders as the *New Yorker* reached a much broader (and more gentile) readership. In particular, the story's depiction of a duplicitous Jewish Army private named Sheldon Grossbart led many Jewish leaders to label Roth as a self-hating Jew, his depiction of unsavory Jewish characters inappropriate coming from a Jewish writer so soon after the Holocaust. In the story, Grossbart attempts to manipulate his superior, Nathan Marx, another Jew, into assuring that Grossbart won't be shipped overseas to fight in the Second World War. Marx ultimately deflects Grossbart's machinations, and the story ends as the young private gets his orders to ship out to the war's Pacific theater. In "Writing about Jews," originally published in *Commentary* in 1963, Roth recounted the criticism the story received, singling out one letter that had charged him with having "done as much harm as all the organized anti-Semitic organizations have done to make people believe that all Jews are cheats, liars, connivers. Your story makes people—the general public—forget all the great Jews who have lived, all the Jewish boys who served well in the armed services, all the Jews who live honest hard lives the world over" (*Why Write?* 58). Another letter from a prominent rabbi read: "What is being done to silence this man? Medieval Jews would have known what to do with him . . ." (59).

In "Writing about Jews," Roth directly responded to the criticism, arguing that the "test of any literary work is not how broad is its range of representation—for all that breadth may be characteristic of a kind of narrative—but the veracity with which the writer reveals what he has chosen to represent" (*Why Write?* 55). Roth's response remains very much in line with the view of literature that had shaped his earliest notions of himself as a novelist—that the writer has no obligations to the community but instead must present reality in all its messiness. Like many of his contemporaries (Ellison, Updike, Mailer, Didion), Roth would privilege the primacy of literature over any familial or group obligations that might be harmed by that fiction. "Informing," Roth calls the underlying offense of which he was accused. "There was the charge so many of the correspondents had made, even when they did not want to make it openly to me, or to themselves. I had informed on the Jews. I had told the Gentiles what apparently it would otherwise have been possible to keep secret from them: that the perils of human nature afflict the members of our minority" (*Why Write?* 59). Reflecting on the controversy in his memoir *The Facts*, Roth singles out a 1962 symposium on "The Crisis of Conscience in Minority Writers of Fiction" at Yeshiva University in New York, where he had been on a panel with Ralph Ellison and Pietro di Donato. The Yeshiva incident would prove to be a formative event in his young career; he would ultimately identify the panel as the moment he "realized that I was not just opposed but hated" by this Jewish audience (127). Although he would later appreciate the hostile reception as pivotal in shaping how his fiction would go on to question the nature of Jewish identity, in the immediate aftermath of the controversy Roth purposely backed away from writing about Jewish life.

This reluctance can be felt in his next two novels, *Letting Go* and *When She Was Good*. Published in 1962, three years after the success of *Goodbye, Columbus*, *Letting Go* stands as the most ambitious of his pre-*Portnoy* works, and it is, not surprisingly, his most overstuffed novel. Coming in at over six hundred pages, *Letting Go*'s plot remains nearly impossible to summarize succinctly: the novel centers on Gabe Wallach, an overly cautious and intelligent young intellectual from a well-to-do Jewish family (his father is a successful dentist in Manhattan), who strives to lead a serious life and slowly discovers the devastating consequences that can come from such an attempt. Much like that other great American innocent, Henry James's Isabel Archer, Gabe ultimately discovers his impotence in successfully navigating a world that seems impervious to reason. The book begins with Gabe, recently discharged from the Army, mulling over a letter that his mother had sent him shortly before her death, in which she confesses to regretting how she felt constrained by her husband. "In my grief and confusion," Gabe observes at the very beginning of the novel, "I promised myself that I would do no violence to human life, not to another's, and not to my own" (3).

As the novel progresses, Gabe slowly allows himself to become involved with other people's problems: first with Paul and Libby Hertz, a young married couple whom he encounters at the University of Iowa, and then with Martha Reganhart, a divorced mother of two with whom Gabe embarks on a troubled relationship. In addition to chronicling Gabe's education, the novel gives a portrait of Paul and Libby's unhappy marriage. The Hertzes are suffering through a mostly miserable union, a history that Roth chronicles in all its wretched glory—from Paul's parents disowning him for marrying outside the Jewish religion, to Libby's abortion, to the health and financial problems that plague them as Paul pursues his graduate degree—in the novel's long second section, entitled "Paul loves Libby." Indeed, *Letting Go* offers a cornucopia of all the dizzying ways in which people can get each other wrong, a theme that dominates much of Roth's later fiction. Fiction, more so than any other narrative medium, can show us *how* people can so misread the world and themselves, and it's this sort of misreading that Roth so masterfully displays in his first novel.

Letting Go nevertheless offers a bleak view of literature's status within American culture during the Eisenhower years. Literature ultimately fails Roth's characters as they struggle to comprehend a world that seems utterly indifferent to the moral intricacies captured in James's fiction. This indifference is especially apparent in the scene, early in the novel, when Gabe travels up to Brooklyn to broker a reconciliation between Paul and his parents. Like almost all of Gabe's actions, his efforts end rather disastrously as Paul's parents appear unmoved. What's most striking about this scene, however, is what happens directly after as Gabe talks with Maury and Doris Horvitz, friends of Paul's from childhood—Doris dated Paul in high school—who now live in the same building as the elder Hertzes. Maury and Doris, in many ways, embody the conventional tastes from which both Gabe and Paul are actively trying to escape. Doris describes herself and her husband as well read because they "get Book of the Month, *Harper's* and *Look*" and she recommends that Gabe and Paul read *Marjorie Morningstar*, the sentimental 1955 novel about a young Jewish woman, which was made into a successful film starring Natalie Wood and Gene Kelly. Even though Doris's conventional tastes run counter to Gabe's James-inflected sensibility, he nonetheless finds her attractive and quickly kisses her. "For a second she looked nothing more than irritated, as though out on a picnic the weather had taken an unexpected turn," Gabe notes of the situation. "But then she bit her lip, and life became, even for Doris, a very threatening affair. Then that passed, too. She turned her back to me. I took my place on the cushion, and for the next five minutes neither of us said anything" (187).

The ambivalence of this encounter nicely illustrates the literary and ethical di-
lemmas the novel so carefully explores. The scene signals the failure of "good"
literature—in this case, the baroque fiction of Henry James—as a safeguard
against desire and moral uncertainty. Literature might capture all our contradictory desires, Roth suggests in the book, but it cannot protect us from those
desires or from the harm we inflict on others.

Inspired by Sherwood Anderson, Theodore Dreiser, and Sinclair Lewis,
When She Was Good continues Roth's move away from the comic deftness of
Goodbye, Columbus as it chronicles the oppressiveness of life in small-town
middle America. The novel remains an anomaly of sorts within Roth's oeuvre:
the book features no Jewish characters, and its restrained prose style reflects
the limitations and dreariness of the lives depicted in the novel. Set in the community of Liberty Center, a small town in an unnamed upper-midwestern state,
during the early 1950s, the novel traces the fairly miserable history of Lucy
Nelson, an intelligent and ambitious young woman whose aspirations for a
better life are thwarted by the men who continually hurt or disappoint her: her
alcoholic father, Duane "Whitey" Nelson, who physically abuses her mother;
her kindly but ineffectual grandfather, Willard Carroll, who enables Whitey's
abusive behavior; her first boyfriend, Roy Bassart, who impregnates her and
then becomes her rather hapless husband; a doctor who refuses to perform an
abortion on her when she is eighteen. In a particularly disturbing sequence,
Roth narrates Roy's violent attempts to force Lucy into having sexual inter-
course: "And then he began to say trust me to her, over and over, and please,
please, and she did not see how she could stop him from doing what he was doing to her without reaching up and sinking her teeth into his throat, which was
directly over her face" (106). The sequence presents an especially brutal version
of the sexual politics of the early 1950s, as Roy both physically and mentally
coerces Lucy into having sex.

Lucy remains, with good reason, convinced of her moral superiority to
those men who continually fail her. After considering converting to Catholi-
cism, a teenaged Lucy, like many of Roth's male protagonists, embraces athe-
ism and remains outraged at the fact of being surrounded by men who are
either morally weak or abusive. "People can call me all the names they want—
I don't care," Lucy thinks to herself. "I have nothing to confess, because I am
right and they are wrong and I will not be destroyed!" (83). It's a sense of moral
indignation that Lucy would share with many of Roth's male protagonists—
the anger that propels Alex Portnoy, for example, as well as Nathan Zuckerman—but coming from a young woman in the 1950s it is viewed as being the
result of hysteria or self-righteousness. Reflecting on the novel in 1984, Roth
defended his characterization of Lucy against charges that the character was

somehow a product of his misogyny, a charge frequently leveled against Roth in the second half of his career: "Lucy Nelson is a furious adolescent who wants a decent life. . . . She happens to be raging against aspects of middle-class American life that the new militant feminism was to identify as the enemy only a few years after Lucy's appearance in print—hers might even be thought of as a case of premature feminist rage." (*Why Write?* 152). Roth's assertion is not as far-fetched as it might first seem—the male-dominated world Lucy finds herself in is, in fact, oppressive and corrosive. That Lucy's anger, her sense of moral indignation, causes her undoing should be emphasized. While many of Roth's male protagonists use their fury as a way of liberating themselves from the constraints of the outside world, Lucy is denied that possibility. At the end of the novel, she has been abandoned by her family and freezes to death in Passion Paradise, her body to be discovered only days later by teenagers visiting the infamous make-out spot. It's an ironic and grim ending, one that reflects the moral seriousness that Roth was straining to achieve with the book.

The dourness and self-conscious seriousness of *When She Was Good*, however, would be spectacularly broken by Roth's next novel, *Portnoy's Complaint*. Released in January 1969, the novel immediately reshaped Roth's career and would make him a literary celebrity. "Rereading *Portnoy's Complaint* forty-five years on," he mused in 2014, "I am shocked and pleased: shocked that I could have been so reckless, pleased to be reminded that I was once so reckless" (*Why Write?* 388). If Roth had not published another novel, *Portnoy's Complaint* would have secured his legacy as one of the most distinctive literary voices of his generation, a master of voice and performance who was able to capture the absurdities of contemporary sexual life. The novel follows the thirty-three-year-old Alexander (Alex) Portnoy, a good Jewish son who has become a successful lawyer and established a civically-minded career as the Assistant Commissioner of Human Opportunity for the City of New York, as he obsessively confesses his lust, his guilt, and his obsession with his childhood (particularly his mother, Sophie, who emerges as an almost caricature of the suffocating Jewish mother). The immediate audience for this confession is Alex's psychoanalyst, Dr. Otto Spielvogel, who remains silent until the novel's final page. Unlike the heavily plotted *Letting Go*, *Portnoy's Complaint* remains largely plotless as Roth's protagonist bounces between his childhood memories of growing up in Newark during the 1940s to his desire to liberate himself from what he sees as the familial and religious constraints that he feels inhibit his sexual satisfaction. "Why must the least deviation from respectable conventions cause me such inner hell," Alex asks his analyst, suggesting the ways he remains deeply controlled by the sense of propriety instilled in him as a boy growing up in Newark. "When I *hate* those fucking conventions! When I know *better* than the taboos! Doctor, my doctor, what do you say, LET'S PUT THE ID BACK IN YID! Liberate this nice Jewish boy's libido, will you please?" (124).

Alex's quest for absolute sexual liberation largely comes in the form of bedding a series of gentile women. Over the course of the book, he recalls his relationships with these *shikses*, all of whom he nicknames: Kay Campbell ("the Pumpkin"), Alex's college girlfriend, a relationship that abruptly ends when Kay admits she won't convert to Judaism if they marry; the wealthy Sarah Abbot Maulsby ("the Pilgrim"), a woman of WASP privilege whose relationship with Alex eventually flounders due to her extreme reluctance to perform oral sex; and Mary Jane Reed ("the Monkey"), the woman Alex was dating right before he entered analysis and whose unflattering nickname stems from Portnoy seeing her eat a banana off the ground. "What I'm saying, Doctor, is that I don't seem to stick my dick up these girls, as much as I stick it up their backgrounds," he admits in one the novel's most famous passages, "as though through fucking I will discover America. *Conquer* America—maybe that's more like it. Columbus, Captain Smith, Governor Winthrop, General Washington—now Portnoy" (235). The aggression here—the emphasis on "conquering America"—is quite telling, revealing not only the anger that pervades Portnoy's sexual relationships but also suggesting his ambivalent relationship to his nation, even as he affirms his status as a real American.

The novel is a sustained comic performance and a riff on the popularity of Freudian analysis, which had come into vogue in the United States over the previous two decades. In his *Paris Review* interview, Roth observed, "The experience of psychoanalysis was probably more useful to me as a writer than as a neurotic, although there may be a false distinction there. It's an experience that I shared with tens of thousands of baffled people, and anything that powerful in the private domain that joins a writer to his generation, to his class, to his moment, is tremendously important for him, providing that afterwards he can separate himself enough to examine the experience objectively, imaginatively, in the writing clinic" (*Why Write?* 149–50). *Portnoy's Complaint*'s engagement with psychoanalysis, along with its reputation for being a "dirty" book, made it something of a cultural phenomenon. By 1975, it "had sold nearly half a million copies in hardback in the United States and three and half million in paperback."[4] Gooblar records that during the first five months of 1969, the *New York Times* featured eleven pieces on Roth, and the novel stayed at the top of the *Times* bestseller list for a remarkable fourteen consecutive weeks.[5]

Alongside John Updike's *Couples* (1968) and Erica Jong's *Fear of Flying* (1973), *Portnoy's Complaint* is ostensibly both a product and reflection of the sexual permissiveness that emerged during the late 1960s as the Sexual Revolution transformed, seemingly overnight, what might be able to be depicted in serious literature; it is not surprising that when the television show *Mad Men* (2007–15) reimagined 1969, it featured a quick scene where that series' oversexed protagonist, Don Draper, reads the novel in his office before quickly tossing it aside so that a co-worker won't catch him with it. Not surprisingly, the novel was read by several critics not only as evidence of Roth's betrayal of his potential as a writer—the literary promise of *Goodbye, Columbus* squandered on extended comic riffs on masturbation—but also as symptomatic of a broader cultural decline. The estimable Diana Trilling, for instance, argued that *Portnoy's Complaint* advanced a larger assault on the culture: "Mr. Roth's funny book is the latest offensive in our escalating literary-political war upon society. And intuitively it has been welcomed as such by most of its reviewers—the popular success of a work often depends as much on its latent as on its overt content."[6]

Trilling's sense of *Portnoy's Complaint* as belonging to the "latest offensive in our escalating literary-political war upon society" seems generous when read next to Irving Howe's "Philip Roth Reconsidered." The essay, published in *Commentary* in 1972, reflects Howe's reversal of his previous endorsement of Roth's talent—he had written a complimentary review of *Goodbye, Columbus*—and the review would severely rankle Roth, who would revisit the incident in *The Anatomy Lesson* (1983) with the critic Milton Appel, a figure clearly modeled on Howe, who writes a devastating review of Nathan Zuckerman's fourth book, *Carnovsky*. Indeed, Howe's review of *Portnoy* both condemns the book and denounces Roth's integrity as a literary artist, as he sees the novel as evidence of Roth's "thin personal culture" and of his desire to appeal to a debased broader readership that values titillation over enlightenment. "The cruelest thing anyone can do with *Portnoy's Complaint* is to read it twice," Howe quips midway through the essay as he pivots from Roth's early fiction to *Portnoy*. "An assemblage of gags strung onto the outcry of an analytic patient, the book thrives best on casual responses; it demands little more from the reader than a nightclub performer demands: a rapid exchange of laugh for punch-line, a breath or two of rest, some variations on the first response, and a quick exit. Such might be the most generous way of discussing *Portnoy's Complaint* were it not for the solemn ecstasies the book has elicited, in line with Roth's own feeling that it constitutes a liberating act for himself, his generation, and maybe the whole culture."[7]

To see *Portnoy's Complaint*, however, as a rejection of the serious literary ambitions of Roth's early work or a straightforward endorsement of the benefits of sexual liberation misreads the novel and its sexual politics.[8] In *The Facts*, Roth recalls the novel's composition as sort of maturation of his literary voice, the product not of a writer abandoning his literary ambitions for cheap

laughs but rather of one who had a found a new form, the psychoanalytic confession, through which to display that voice in all its humor and rage. "It was a
book that had rather less to do with 'freeing' me from my Jewishness or from
my family (the purpose divined by many, who were convinced by the evidence
of *Portnoy's Complaint* that the author had to be on bad terms with both),"
Roth writes in *The Facts*, "than with liberating me from an apprentice's literary models, particularly from the awesome graduate-school authority of Henry
James, whose *[The] Portrait of a Lady* had been a virtual handbook during the
early drafts of *Letting Go*, and from the example of Flaubert, whose detached
irony in the face of a small-town woman's disastrous delusions had me obsessively thumbing through the pages of *Madame Bovary* during those years I
was searching for the perch from which to observe the people in *When She Was
Good*" (156–7).[9] While he freed himself from the "graduate-school authority
of Henry James," Roth nevertheless insisted on *Portnoy's Complaint*'s literary
credentials. Responding to George Plimpton's inquiry in a 1969 interview as to
whether or not Lenny Bruce's stand-up routine influenced the crafting of Portnoy's comic monologues, Roth flatly rejected the notion, noting he "was more
strongly influenced by a stand-up comic named Franz Kafka and a very funny
bit he does called 'The Metamorphosis.'" (*Why Write?* 69).

Roth would later frame Alex Portnoy's confession as a reflection of the
rhetorical outlandishness, the theatricality, that defined the political rhetoric
of the late 1960s, as many Americans protested the Vietnam War. Recounting
the factors that had shaped *Portnoy's Complaint*, Roth in *The Facts* highlights
the political fervor of the antiwar movement, "the ferocity of the rebellious
rhetoric unleashed against the president and his war, the assault that [Lyndon]
Johnson's own seething cornball bravado inspired and from which even he,
with his rich and randy vein of linguistic contempt, had eventually to flee in
defeat, as though before a deluge of verbal napalm" (137–8). The performativity of Portnoy's confession to Spielvogel, his compulsive need to act out,
seemingly relishing in performing his rage, suggests the ways in which the
narrative remains deeply informed by the volatile political environment of
the late 1960s. At one moment in the novel, Alex recalls his childhood love of
the Chinese National Anthem: "And then my favorite line, commencing as it
does with my favorite word in the English language: *In*-dig-*na*-tion fills the
hearts of all out our coun-try-*men!* A-*rise!* A-*rise!* A-RISE!' (169). That Alex
Portnoy would embrace the word "indignation" as his favorite nicely captures
the sense of rage that fuels the novel (and not surprisingly, Roth would title his
2008 novel *Indignation*, suggesting his own fondness for the word). "Whew!
Have I got grievances," Alex muses earlier in the book. "Do I harbor hatreds
I didn't even know were there! Is it the process, Doctor, or is it what we call

'the material'? All I do is complain, the repugnance seems bottomless, and I'm beginning to wonder if maybe enough isn't enough" (94).

Such lines reinforce the impotence of Portnoy's talk: for all his ranting, he remains unable to free himself from the sense of morality—the social and sexual inhibitions—that his parents instilled in him as a child growing up in Newark. The novel, in the end, is about the impossibility of truly liberating the self, a failure that becomes especially apparent in the novel's disturbing final section. *Portnoy's Complaint* is less a record of the freewheeling 1960s, the promise of free love and unbridled sexual license, and more a rejection of that myth as Alex remains unable to divorce himself from the sense of morality and community bonds that have shaped his sense of himself and the outer world. In the novel's final section, Alex recalls a recent trip to Israel where he meets Naomi, "The Jewish Pumpkin," a twenty-one-year-old Israeli who "after completing her Army service . . . decided not to return to the kibbutz where she had been born and raised, but instead to join a commune of young native-born Israelis clearing boulders of black volcanic rock from a barren settlement in the mountains overlooking the boundary with Syria" (258). An affirmed socialist, Naomi sees Alex as a product of a sick and unjust nation. Citing the quiz show scandals of the late 1950s, a controversy that Roth would later revisit in *Zuckerman Unbound*, Naomi debunks Alex's sense of himself as a valuable public servant: "You are not the enemy of the system. You are not even a challenge to the system, as you seem to think. You are only one of its policemen, a paid employee, an accomplice" (262). Naomi's stance on America is worth emphasizing as it deflates Alex's patriotic sense of his nation, a patriotism that Alex admits is a byproduct of the World War II propaganda that informed his childhood. The encounter with Naomi accelerates Alex's unraveling: he attempts to have sex with her, even to sexually assault her, but is rendered impotent as the physically imposing Naomi competently fends him off.

After confessing this failure, Alex concludes his session by fantasizing that he is being hunted down by the cops for his crimes before letting out a "pure howl" (273). Alex's prolonged primal scream leads to the famous "punch line" that concludes the narrative, "So [*said the doctor*]. Now vee may perhaps to begin. Yes?" (274). The lines, the only words spoken by Spielvogel throughout the novel, suggest that the foregoing prolonged monologue has not resolved Alex's issues, but instead has been the necessary prelude to the actual work of analysis. Yet, the novel would also seem to undercut the effectiveness of psychoanalysis as a way of understanding the self. Bernard Avishai suggests the novel's concluding lines "signal that Spielvogel is fair game, too—that Roth's many-layered satire is of psychoanalytic orthodoxy."[10] Ultimately, *Portnoy's Complaint* marks Roth's first sustained foray into the notion of the performative self—a notion that he would return to with more intellectual force in later novels such as *The Counterlife* and *Operation Shylock*—and establish the unrestrained, uncompromising voice that would define much of Roth's subsequent fiction. With its willingness to burrow into the darkest aspects of the self, its capacity to admit and even relish the most unsavory of thoughts or impulses, *Portnoy's Complaint* would seem to anticipate the inward turn that American culture would take at the onset of the 1970s as the nation attempted to grapple with the trauma of the previous decade.

Portnoy's Complaint would also establish the more outrageous narratives that would characterize Roth's fiction for the next five years. Speaking of his baseball farce *The Great American Novel*, Roth noted: "All sorts of impulses that I might once have put down as excessive, frivolous, or exhibitionistic I allowed to surface and proceed to their destination. The idea was to see what would emerge if everything that was 'a little too' at first glance was permitted to go all the way. I understood that disaster might ensue (I have been informed by some that it did), but I tried to put my faith in the fun that I was having. *Writing as pleasure*. Enough to make Flaubert spin in his grave" (*Why Write?* 121). This assessment accurately describes the outlandish fiction that Roth published in the immediate wake of *Portnoy's Complaint*'s massive commercial success. In *The Breast*, the first entry in the Kepesh trilogy, Roth offers his own take on Kafka's "The Metamorphosis" as David Kepesh, a professor of comparative literature, wakes up one morning having been transformed into a gigantic human breast.[11] The short story "On the Air," which appeared in the *New American Review* in 1970, is even more extreme, a work so grotesque that Roth never collected it in any of his books. The long story, set during the Second World War, centers on a talent agent named Milton Lippman who wants to recruit Albert Einstein to be part of a radio quiz show. The story soon dissolves into a surrealistic nightmare as Lippman visits a tavern where he encounters a series of violent figures that reflect Lippman's "repressed anxieties about his position as a Jew" living in the United States.[12] In what stands as probably the strangest moment in all of Roth, the story depicts a soda jerk who has an ice cream scoop for a hand sodomizing the police chief, upon the request of The Chief, with his scoop hand. Roth writes that the "blood [The Chief] still had in him [was] trickling from his rectum, and [he was] dragging behind the imprisoned soda jerk, as though he were some one-armed appendage growing from The Chief's body" (48).[13] His other short work of the period, "'I Always Wanted You to Admire My Fasting'; or, Looking at Kafka," written in 1973 and collected in *Reading Myself and Others* (1975), continued the fascination with Kafka evident in *The Breast*. The first half of "Looking at Kafka" presents Roth's meditations on the writer; the second half is a short story in which Kafka survives and emigrates to Newark, where he becomes Roth's Hebrew teacher and briefly dates his Aunt Rhoda, a precursor to the counterhistories that Roth will go on to write in *The Ghost Writer* and *The Plot Against America*.

Our Gang, a vicious satire of the Nixon administration that takes its title from the beloved children's film serial that was produced from 1922 until 1944, best displays Roth's humor at its most unhinged. In his review of the novel for the *New York Times*, Dwight McDonald described *Our Gang* as "far-fetched, unfair, tasteless, disturbing, logical, coarse and very funny—I laughed out loud 16 times and giggled internally a statistically unverifiable amount. In short, a masterpiece."[14] The brief novel returns to the extreme methods evident in "On the Air" as Roth pillories the hypocritical moralizing of Richard Nixon: the book opens with President Tricky E. Dixon speculating whether Lieutenant William Calley, the officer convicted of the 1968 My Lai massacre, was guilty of performing abortions when murdering innocent Vietnamese women (5–6), and the novel concludes with an assassinated Dixon running to be elected head Devil. During the course of the book, Dixon contemplates extending the right to vote to fetuses as a way of expanding his political power and later instigates a riot, instigated by the Boy Scouts, after denying he supports sexual inter-course; he later blames the riot on the baseball player Curt Flood, the former St. Louis Cardinals all-star who sued Major League Baseball in 1970 to avoid being traded—the case, which Flood lost, that eventually led to the creation of free agency. The Boy Scouts' riot, in rather absurd fashion, triggers Dixon to start a war with Denmark as way of deflecting bad press.

Roth is clearly having fun in these works—*Our Gang* perfectly captures Nixon's shameless pandering rhetoric—but these are ultimately slighter entries in his oeuvre, revealing his uncertainty as to how to move forward after the success of *Portnoy's Complaint*. His longer novels of this period, *The Great American Novel* and *My Life as a Man*, are more substantial, anticipating the thematic issues and the narrative experiments that he would pursue in his sub-sequent work. *The Great American Novel*, published the year of the Watergate hearings, remains Roth's most underappreciated novel, combining a genuine love of baseball with the historiographic questions that Roth would pursue more seriously two decades later in the American Trilogy. Part screwball com-edy, part reflection on how history is constructed, *The Great American Novel* is narrated by the eighty-seven-year-old ex-journalist playfully named Word "Smitty" Smith, who follows the fictional Patriot League's woeful Ruppert Mundys. For all its fantastic jokes, the Patriot League falls apart after a former pitcher turned Soviet spy named Gil Gamesh falsely implicates the league as a hotbed of Communist activity and a threat to national security. In retrospect, the novel offers Roth's first attempt to illustrate what he terms, in *Reading Myself and Others* (1975), as the "demythologizing decade" of the 1960s: "I mean by this that much that had previously been considered in my own brief lifetime to be disgraceful and disgusting forced itself upon the national consciousness, loathsome or not; what was assumed to be beyond reproach became the target of blasphemous assault; what was imagined to be indestructible, impermeable, in the very nature of American things, yielded and collapsed overnight" (87–8).

Published two years after *The Great American Novel*, *My Life as a Man* also ranks as one of Roth's most overlooked novels. It not only introduces the character of Nathan Zuckerman, who would go on to become Roth's most prominent alter-ego, but also points ahead to the narrative experiments that he would pursue in *The Counterlife* and *Operation Shylock*. The novel also anticipates works of autofiction, such as Karl Ove Knausgaard's *My Struggle* (2014), Nell Zink's *The Wallcreeper* (2014), and Ben Lerner's *10:04* (2014), that came into critical vogue in the twenty-first century. Comprised of two of Peter Tarnopol's short stories—collected in a section entitled "Useful Fictions"—and a longer section of Tarnopol's autobiographical musings ("My True Story"), the novel traces Tarnopol's disastrous marriage to Maureen Johnson, in Tarnopol's words a *"barmaid, an abstract painter, a sculptress, a waitress, an actress (what an actress!), a short-story writer, a liar, and a psychopath"* (99). The long novel remains Roth's most direct attempt to come to terms with his tumultuous first marriage to Margaret Martinson Williams, whom he met while a graduate instructor at the University of Chicago. They married in 1959, the same year *Goodbye, Columbus* was published, and their union ended only when Williams was killed in an automobile accident in 1968, after years of hindering their divorce proceedings. Roth would consistently view their relationship as the major trauma of his young adulthood. Writing a few years later in *The Facts*, Roth describes *My Life as a Man* as his attempt "to demonstrate that my imaginative faculties had managed to outlive the waste of all that youthful strength, that I'd not only survived the consequences of my devastating case of moral simpletonism but finally prevailed over my grotesque deference to what this wretched small-town gentile paranoid defined as my humane, my manly—yes, even my Jewish—duty" (108). Later in *The Facts*, Nathan Zuckerman challenges Roth's presentation of his first marriage. "If you want to reminisce productively," Zuckerman informs his creator, "maybe what you should be writing, instead of autobiography, are thirty thousand words from Josie's [Roth's name for Williams in the work] point of view. *My Life as a Woman. My Life as a Woman with That Man*" (175).

My Life as a Man, however, should not be read purely as confession or as a roman à clef of Roth and Williams's relationship: it interrogates the impetus behind autobiographical writing, questioning whether there is an irreducible self that is capable of being reflected in narrative. In his *Paris Review* interview, Roth noted how the novel "diverges so dramatically in so many places from its origin in my own nasty situation that I'm hard put, some twenty-five year later, to sort out the invention of 1975 from the facts of 1959. You might as well ask the author of [Norman Mailer's World War II novel] *The Naked and the Dead* what happened to him in the Philippines" (*Why Write?* 150). The novel nevertheless largely follows the trajectory, if not the exact details, of Roth's first marriage. Tarnopol attempts to understand, first through the two stories presented in the "Useful Fictions" section of the novel, and then through the autobiographical writing that constitutes the bulk of the novel, what led him to marry Maureen. Another patient of Dr. Spielvogel, the doctor last seen in *Portnoy's Complaint*, Tarnopol struggles to comprehend what propelled his decision to marry the troubled Maureen. His project is explicitly solipsistic. Recalling how his marriage played out before the tumult of the 1960s, Peter recounts that

> the newspapers and the nightly television news began to depict an increasingly chaotic America and to bring news of bitter struggles for freedom and power which made my personal difficulties with alimony payments and inflexible divorce laws appear by comparison to be inconsequential. Unfortunately, these highly visible dramas of social disorder and human misery did nothing whatsoever to mitigate my obsession; to the contrary, that the most vivid and momentous history since World War Two was being made in the streets around me, day by day, *hour by hour*, only caused me to feel even more isolated by my troubles from the world at large, more embittered by the narrow and guarded life I now felt called upon to live—or able to live—because of my brief, misguided foray into matrimony. (268–9)

Not surprisingly, the novel is Roth's most vitriolic, its rage providing ammunition to critics who labeled Roth a misogynist. Nevertheless, *My Life as a Man* remains significant for how it examines the connection between narrative and selfhood, a connection that Roth would explore more fully in his later fiction. Its narrative experiments—the stories embedded within yet another story; the deliberate conflation of fact and fiction—suggest the postmodern playfulness that Roth would embrace as he transformed his fiction during the next two decades of his career. As Debra Shostak has argued, the novel "anticipates poststructural commonplaces about identity" while also questioning the possibility of autobiographical writing, insinuating that "there is no self to write, at least not as a stable entity with presence in the world that can be mirrored in language."[15] Despite its somewhat obscure place in his oeuvre, *My Life as a Man* marks a fitting conclusion to the first stage of Roth's career, grappling with what Roth perceived as the pivotal decision that had derailed his young adult life while also opening up new narrative possibilities, ones that he would reap more fully when he returned to the character of Nathan Zuckerman a few years later in *The Ghost Writer* (1979).

CHAPTER 3

The Writing Life

Zuckerman Bound, The Counterlife, and *Exit Ghost*

In the concluding section of Roth's 1988 autobiography *The Facts*, Nathan Zuckerman, the fictional writer whose life and career Roth chronicled for over thirty years, responds to his creator's decision to abandon fiction for the seemingly more transparent form of autobiography: "I owe everything to you, while you, however, owe me nothing less than the freedom to write freely. I am your permission, your indiscretion, the key to disclosure. I understand that now as I never did before" (161–2). While charmingly self-serving, Zuckerman's argument for his necessity more broadly suggests the character's importance to Roth's most successful fiction. Starting with *My Life as a Man*, where he debuted as the invention of that novel's writer-protagonist Peter Tarnopol, Nathan Zuckerman would appear, either as the protagonist or the narrator, of nine more books.[1] On Zuckerman's appeal, Roth observed in his 1984 *Paris Review* interview with Hermione Lee, "[Zuckerman] has two dominant modes: his mode of self-abnegation, and his fuck-'em mode. You want a bad Jewish boy, that's what you're going to get. He rests from one by taking up the other, though, as we see, it's not much of a rest. The thing about Zuckerman that interests me is that everybody's split, but few so openly as this" (*Why Write?* 145).

This division appears most apparent in the first four Zuckerman books— *The Ghost Writer* (1979), *Zuckerman Unbound* (1981), *The Anatomy Lesson* (1983), and *The Prague Orgy* (1985)—a sequence that Roth published in one volume in 1985 as *Zuckerman Bound*. Through the course of the series, Roth traces the major events of the protagonist's professional career, from the innocent young writer presented in *The Ghost Writer* to the exhausted and pain-racked middle-aged man captured in *The Anatomy Lesson* and *The Prague*

Orgy. "A writer learns to stay around, has to, in order to make sense of incurable life, in order to chart the turnings of the punishing unknown even where there's no sense to be made," Roth writes in *The Anatomy Lesson* as Zuckerman experiences a midlife crisis of sorts (111). Roth would return to the character the year after the publication of *The Prague Orgy* in the mind-bending *The Counterlife* (1986), his most potent examination of the interrelationship between narrative and identity. In the American Trilogy—*American Pastoral* (1997), *I Married a Communist* (1998), and *The Human Stain* (2000)—Zuckerman moves beyond imagining himself and considers the lives of other men and, more broadly, the trajectory of the United States in the decades following the Second World War. After employing Zuckerman as the narrative imagination behind the American Trilogy, Roth would revisit the character one final time in 2007's *Exit Ghost*, depicting Zuckerman reentering public life after more than a decade of living in seclusion.

This chapter will focus on the novels—the Zuckerman Bound series, *The Counterlife*, and *Exit Ghost*—in which Zuckerman appears as the primary actor within the narrative. Over the course of these books, Roth gives Zuckerman much of his own biography and career trajectory: an idyllic childhood in the Weequahic section of Newark; leaving that beloved home for college; a brief stint in the Army; graduate work at the University of Chicago; early success publishing fiction that scandalizes the Jewish American community; a sexually explicit bestseller (called *Carnovsky*) that results in celebrity and notoriety. The differences between Zuckerman and Roth are subtle, but worth noting: Zuckerman has a younger brother, Henry, who struggles with his older brother's penchant for cannibalizing his family's life for his fiction (in reality, Roth had a close relationship with his older brother, Sandy, whom he had idolized during their childhood); Zuckerman's father enjoys professional and financial success as a podiatrist while Roth's worked hard to carve out a stable lower-middle-class existence as an insurance broker; Zuckerman's father recoils from his son's fiction while Roth's parents were proud of his accomplishments; Zuckerman is married and divorced several times over while Roth married only twice.

Beyond simply playing an unsolvable game of mirrors with readers, the Zuckerman novels rigorously explore the ethical implications of the writing life, a concern at the forefront of *The Ghost Writer*. Published in 1979 and dedicated to Milan Kundera, the Czech novelist whom Roth had befriended through his work as editor for Penguin's "Writers from the Other Europe" series, *The Ghost Writer* launched the second half of Roth's career and marked his most substantial critical success since *Portnoy's Complaint*. In both form and content, *The Ghost Writer* anticipates the more expansive novels that Roth would publish in the 1980s and 1990s, but in its concision and pungency it stands as one of his most substantial achievements. The novel reintroduces Nathan Zuckerman, whom readers first encountered as the fictional alter-ego of Peter Tarnopol in *My Life as a Man*. The Zuckerman who appears in *The Ghost Writer*, however, seems to be a new incarnation of the character. Claudia Roth Pierpont observes that "the new Zuckerman is entirely different from that maritally entrapped and often enraged figure, as he is different from Peter Tarnopol and David Kepesh, who have also been maritally entrapped and enraged—just like Philip Roth."[2] Roth's reclamation of Zuckerman in *The Ghost Writer* reflects the more flexible approach to character that he developed during the second half of his career. Unlike John Updike in his Rabbit Angstrom tetralogy, where Updike meticulously chronicles the life-and-times of Harry "Rabbit" Angstrom, Roth appears to have very little interest in constructing a definitive or consistent history for Zuckerman.[3] Instead, the character can be better understood as a constellation of biographical circumstances (many of which he shares with his creator) and a certain narrative sensibility—what Roth in a 2000 interview described as a "dark Zuckerman take on American life"—that animates the series.[4]

The Ghost Writer begins with Zuckerman, twenty-three years old and fresh off the success of his first published stories, as he spends the weekend with one of his literary idols, E. I. Lonoff.[5] Over the course of the weekend, Nathan finds himself absorbed into the drama of Lonoff's domestic life as he studies the interplay between Lonoff's wife, Hope, and his young assistant and lover, Amy Bellette, with whom Zuckerman also becomes infatuated. In Lonoff, Zuckerman finds not only a model for the sort of literary life he imagines—a life tending to the production of morally scrupulous fiction—but also a father figure to supplant his own more worldly father, who cannot comprehend his oldest son's penchant for repurposing family history into fiction. Zuckerman, looking back on the events of that weekend from an undisclosed amount of distance, recalls the immediacy of his desire to be anointed Lonoff's literary heir: "For I had come, you see, to submit myself for candidacy as nothing less than E. I. Lonoff's spiritual son, to petition for his moral sponsorship and to win, if I could, the magical protection of his advocacy and his love. Of course, I had a loving father of my own, whom I could ask the world of any day of the week, but my father was a foot doctor and not an artist, and lately we had been having serious trouble in the family because of a new story of mine" (9–10).

The story in question, "Higher Education," as Pierpont notes, resembles many of the stories in *Goodbye, Columbus* since Zuckerman uses an old family scandal regarding an inheritance to present a richly ironic portrait of contemporary Jewish American life.[6] "Nathan, your story, as far as Gentiles are concerned, is about one thing and one thing only," Zuckerman's father, Victor,

argues as he struggles to convince Nathan of the damage his story might bring
to his family and, more broadly, the Jewish American community. "Listen to
me, before you go. It is about kikes. Kikes and their love of money. That is all
our good Christian friends will see. I guarantee you" (94). This battle is at the
center of the book's second section, "Nathan Dedalus," a reference to Stephen
Dedalus, the anguished young writer who is the protagonist of James Joyce's *A
Portrait of the Artist as a Young Man* (1916) and a major character in *Ulysses*
(1922). This nod to Joyce is characteristic of the intertextual approach that
Roth pursues throughout the Zuckerman books and, more vitally, suggests the
somewhat ironic view through which Roth imagines Nathan's struggles as a
young writer in *The Ghost Writer*. "This story isn't us, and what is worse, it
isn't even *you*," Zuckerman's father insists. "You are a loving boy. I watched
you like a hawk all day. I've watched you all your life. You are a good and kind
and considerate young man. You are not somebody who writes this kind of
story and pretends it's the truth" (94–5). "But I *did* write it," Nathan retorts,
suggesting his proclivity for seeing himself as both the good Jewish son—he
had originally shared the story with his father because he wanted to bask in
his approval for this accomplishment—and as a serious writer able to separate
himself from the emotional entanglements of his family and his ethnic community (95).

The fight escalates when his father recruits a family friend, Judge Leopold
Wapter, to write a letter to dissuade Nathan from publishing the story. The
episode, which mirrors the accusations of Jewish self-hatred that Roth received in the aftermath of *Goodbye, Columbus*, illustrates *The Ghost Writer*'s
broader interest in the ethical implications of literature, of the ways in which
art shapes public life. At the end of the letter, Wapter attaches a series of questions—most pointedly, "If you had been living in Nazi Germany in the thirties,
would you have written such a story?"—meant to convince Zuckerman of the
damage his story might do (102). Incidentally, Roth acknowledges in *The Facts*
that Wapter's question came directly from one Roth had been asked at a 1962
symposium at Yeshiva University, where he had been assailed for his depiction
of Jewish life (127). In reimagining this experience, Roth uses it to rip open the
questions regarding the ethical obligations of the writer and the ways in which
art might affect an audience. Such questions are vital to all the Zuckerman
books—by the time of the American Trilogy, Roth considers the ways in which
fictional narratives are integral to our understanding of history—but they are
most acutely imagined in *The Ghost Writer*.

In contrast to his father's emotionality, Nathan earnestly believes art to be
the antidote to the chaos that pervades his life—literature giving meaningful
shape to the inchoate nature of experience. This faith is vital for understanding

his notion of the literary life and how he imagines himself as a young man striving to break free from the constraints imposed by his family. Observing a passage from a Henry James story, "The Middle Years," that Lonoff keeps pinned to a board behind his work desk ("We work in the dark—we do what we can—we give what we have. Our doubt is our passion and our passion is our task. The rest is the madness of art."), Zuckerman appears puzzled by the notion that art somehow is madness: "I would have thought the madness of everything but art. The art was sane, no? Or was I missing something?" (77). Roth's selection of "The Middle Years" as the spark that ignites Zuckerman's imagination is not accidental: the story reflects the questions regarding authorship and the unintended effects that a literary text might occasion. In it, an aging novelist Dencombe is "convalescing from a debilitating ailment at an English health resort when a copy of his latest book, *The Middle Years*, arrives from his publisher" (*Ghost* 113). While at the resort, Dencombe encounters a physician, Dr. Hugh, who becomes so enamored with the novel that he ends up forfeiting his inheritance from a wealthy baroness to be close to the novelist. Dencombe is at first horrified that his novel has had such an unintended impact on Dr. Hugh, but then assuages himself with the idea that "our doubt is our passion and our passion our task. The rest is the madness of art," a conclusion that embraces the many and unpredictable ways in which a work of literature might be used (116). James's conclusion does not so much align with the rather moralistic and simplistic model of reading that Judge Wapter endorses, but it instead embraces a much more fluid, and indeed playful, notion of how literature affects readers. As Patrick Hayes argues in his perceptive reading of this moment, the ambiguity of the James story—how Dencombe accepts the power that fiction might have, how art can occasion unintended and impossible-to-predict consequences—would seem to reflect Roth's own ambitions for *The Ghost Writer*.[7]

After reading the story, Zuckerman overhears Bellette attempting to seduce Lonoff—"Oh, Manny, would it kill you just to kiss my breasts," Bellette asks the reserved writer (120)—a seduction that Lonoff reluctantly refuses, but the implication is that they have had a long-standing sexual relationship. "Oh, if only I could have imagined the scene I'd overheard," Zuckerman exclaims after Lonoff has returned to his marital bed. "If I only I could invent as presumptuously as real life! If one day I could just *approach* the originality and excitement of what actually goes on! But if I ever did, what then would they think of me, my father and his judge? How would my elders hold up against that?" (121). The swirling mixture of events—Zuckerman's desire for Bellette which led to his masturbating in Lonoff's office, the reading of the James story, the fight with his father and Wapter, the overheard encounter between Bellette and

Lonoff, his mother's mentioning of the Broadway production of *The Diary of Anne Frank*—all converge in the novel's third and most spectacular section, "Femme Fatale," where Zuckerman imagines Bellette to be Anne Frank. Here, Zuckerman constructs a credible alternate history for Frank, imagining a life where she escapes the Netherlands and ends up living in the United States. Having escaped the Nazis, she assumes the name Amy Bellette and watches as her diary become the most celebrated artifact of the Holocaust's incalculable loss. Roth's decision to set *The Ghost Writer* in 1956 and not 1959, when he had his first conflict with the Jewish American religious community over the publication of *Goodbye, Columbus,* would seem to be a deliberate choice. David Gooblar points out that "Frances Goodrich and Albert Hackett's adaptation of *The Diary of Anne Frank* opened at the Cort Theater on Broadway in October of 1955, and by setting the book in 1956, when the play was still running, Roth can incorporate it into his story."[8] It is not surprising that Roth has Judge Wapter cite the play at the end of his letter to Zuckerman, calling it "an unforgettable experience" (102), as the drama offered a sanitized version of Frank's *Diary* that, as Gooblar points out, had Anne "actually playing down the suffering of the Jews and essentially equating European Jews in the Holocaust with all persecuted groups throughout history."[9]

Recalling *The Ghost Writer* in a 2014 interview, Roth remarked that in rewriting Frank's history he wanted "to imagine, if not the girl herself—I wanted to imagine that too, though in ways that others had ignored—the function the girl had come to perform in the minds of her vast following of receptive readers" (*Why Write?* 375). By inhabiting an alternate history of Anne Frank, who was only four years older than Roth, Zuckerman considers the repercussions of the Holocaust, insisting on the historical circumstances that enabled it to occur in Europe and not in the United States. "We are not the wretched of Belsen," Zuckerman yells at his mother during the fight over Wapter's letter. "We were not the victims of that crime!" (106). Citing this moment, Gooblar remarks that Zuckerman's version of Anne Frank "counters the approach to Jewish writing suggested by his father and Judge Wapter by always emphasizing the particular context that is relevant."[10] Yet, Zuckerman's mother's response in this exchange—"But we *could* be—in their place we *would* be. Nathan, violence is nothing new to the Jews, you *know* that!" (106)—should not be discounted, as it anticipates the emphasis on fate, on the ways in which the contingencies of history can shape (or destroy) a life, that would become the subject of so much of Roth's later fiction. Beyond considering the meaning of the Holocaust, "Femme Fatale" enables Zuckerman to return to the literary questions provoked by his reading of "The Middle Years" and the ways in which his own fiction has so enflamed his father and the judge. *The Diary* of *Anne Frank* becomes, for Zuckerman, an example *par excellence* of how a writer could never imagine the ways in which her work might be received or used by an audience. Not surprisingly, Zuckerman's Frank counters the sanitized, ever optimistic girl depicted in Goodrich and Hackett's adaptation. In the end, Zuckerman has Anne/Amy keep her identity secret, not so much because she realizes the inspirational aspects of the *Diary* will be lost if she were alive and not dead, but to respect all the voices that have been silenced by Nazi atrocities.

After breaking through his own writer's block, Zuckerman awakens the next morning to witnesses a scene between Lonoff and his long-suffering wife where Hope threatens to leave the marriage. "There is his religion of art, my young successor: rejecting life," Hope warns Amy. "*Not* living is what he makes his beautiful fiction *out* of!" (174–5). Hope's warning echoes throughout the rest of the series, as Zuckerman wrestles with both the social consequences that the writing life entails and how his devotion to his art irrevocably alters his personal relationships. "I'll be curious to see how we all come out someday," Lonoff muses to Zuckerman in the novel's final page. "It could be an interesting story. You're not so nice and polite in your fiction" (180). Lonoff's verdict serves as a perfectly playful ending for a book that has been invested in exploring how literary texts are produced and consumed—for what we have been reading is exactly what Zuckerman has made all of them.

The question of Nathan's essential "niceness" takes center stage in the next two novels of the series, *Zuckerman Unbound* and *The Anatomy Lesson*. Set in 1969, the same year that *Portnoy's Complaint* appeared, *Zuckerman Unbound* captures Nathan Zuckerman as he experiences the aftershocks of having published a sexually explicit bestseller, the aptly named *Carnovsky*. The novel makes Zuckerman a millionaire and a celebrity of sorts, with readers confusing him for his infamous character. "They had mistaken impersonation for confession and were calling out to a character who lived in a book," Zuckerman says of the way strangers would identify him as Carnovsky. "Zuckerman tried taking it as praise—he had made real people believe Carnovsky real too—but in the end he pretended he was only himself, and with his quick, small steps hurried on" (10–1). *Zuckerman Unbound* extends the playful games that propelled *The Ghost Writer*. The novel depicts what on the surface appears to be a barely disguised meditation on the celebrity that Roth experienced in the wake of *Portnoy's Complaint*, with Roth openly inviting readers to confuse fiction for "confession" while also castigating them for that very same impulse. In a particularly amusing episode, Zuckerman receives a photograph of a "young New Jersey secretary" capturing her "reclining in black underwear on her back lawn in Livingston, reading a novel by John Updike," who in 1968 published his own famous sexually explicit novel, *Couples* (58). "Zuckerman studied the photograph on and off for the better part of a morning," Roth writes, "before forwarding it to Massachusetts, along with a note asking if Updike would be good enough to reroute photographs of Zuckerman readers mistakenly sent to him" (58). The episode is typical of the games that Roth plays with readers in *Zuckerman Unbound*—Roth and Updike, by the late 1960s, had established a friendly relationship—encouraging readers to confuse Zuckerman for Roth, fiction for unadulterated confession.[11]

In an essay on *Zuckerman Unbound*, Donald M. Kartiganer observes that it "is not about how a book comes to be, but what happens to a book in the world, how the responses to that book become a mirror of its creative mode and a fertile provocation that generates the next fiction."[12] Nathan's yearning for a literary father has been supplanted by his desire to escape his audience and the ways it misreads his work. Not surprisingly, Nathan's chief sparring partner in the novel is a reader, Alvin Pepler, an obsessed fan and fellow Newarker who gained notoriety a decade earlier when he was involved in a scandal on the television quiz show *Smart Money*. Pepler appears to be modeled on Herb Stempel, who became embroiled in the rigging of the *Twenty-One* quiz show in 1956. Pepler approaches Zuckerman not only to express his fandom—in their initial meeting, he calls Zuckerman Newark's Marcel Proust for the ways in which his novels captured the Newark of their youth (13)—but also for helping write his life story, a book intended to redeem him in the wake of the *Smart Money* scandal. Indeed, Pepler's request anticipates the work that Zuckerman would embark on in the American Trilogy, where he uses other men's lives as a way of imagining America's post-1945 history. *Zuckerman Unbound*, however, shows a more reluctant and self-obsessed Zuckerman. While he finds Pepler to be a fascinating and frightening subject—late in the novel, provoked by Pepler, Zuckerman finds himself writing "steadily for an hour," breaking through the writer's block he has experienced since publishing *Carnovsky* (119)—Zuckerman remains too caught up in the drama of his own life to be able to immerse himself in Pepler's existence.

Zuckerman's tendency to focus on himself seems reasonable when one considers how his existence has been radically altered by the commercial success of *Carnovsky*. The violently carnivalesque environment of the late 1960s would seem to be an especially dangerous time to publish a book with the potential to outrage and offend its audience, a fact that Zuckerman appears all too aware of at the beginning of the novel:

> Vietnam was a slaughterhouse, and off the battlefield as well as on, many
> Americans had gone berserk. Just about a year before, Martin Luther King

and Robert Kennedy had been gunned down by assassins. Closer to home, a former teacher of Zuckerman's was still hiding out because a rifle had been fired at him through his kitchen window as he'd been sitting at his table one night with a glass of warm milk and a Wodehouse novel. The retired bachelor had taught Middle English at the University of Chicago for thirty-five years. The course had been hard, though not that hard. But a bloody nose wasn't enough anymore. Blowing people apart seemed to have replaced the roundhouse punch in the daydreams of the aggrieved: only annihilation gave satisfaction that lasted. (7–8)

Zuckerman's reflections on the chaos of the late 1960s anticipate the questions that he pursues more robustly, and with the benefit of a more fully formed historical perspective, in *American Pastoral*. As Zuckerman suggests, by 1969 actual violence has supplanted social ostracism and censorship as a mode of silencing a writer. Nathan's observations here seem typical of how the early Zuckerman novels engage history, as Roth seems less interested in exploring the meaning of this history, as he later would in the American Trilogy. Instead, Roth employs it as a staging ground for better understanding Zuckerman's sense of himself, the chaos of those years becoming a metaphor for Nathan's inner turmoil—the chaos of the outer world of 1969 reflecting his internal strife. Later in the novel, Pepler accosts Zuckerman for ignoring the consequences of the 1967 Newark riots that radically altered the city's landscape and severely damaged its national reputation. "Newark is bankruptcy! Newark is ashes! Newark is rubble and filth! Own a car in Newark and then you'll find out what Newark's all about! Then you can write *ten* books about Newark! They slit your throat for your radial tires! They cut off both balls for a Bulova watch! And your dick for the fun of it, if it's white," Pepler says of Newark in the aftermath of the riots, suggesting how Zuckerman has ignored the current condition of his beloved hometown (156). A comparable, if less racist, outrage afflicts Zuckerman's father as he spends his time writing aggrieved letters to Lyndon Johnson and then Hubert Humphrey urging them to stop the war in Vietnam, a collection of letters "nearly as fat as *War and Peace*" (177).

But if the political turmoil of 1969 creeps into the margins of the novel, *Zuckerman Unbound* concludes with Nathan losing his own history when his father dies. The sequence describing Victor Zuckerman's death remains one of the most moving portions of the series: "His soft, misty gaze somehow grew enormous, bending their images and drawing them to him like a convex mirror. His chin was quivering—not from the frustrated effort of speech but from the recognition that all effort was pointless now. And it had been the most effortful life. Being Victor Zuckerman was no job you took lightly" (181–2). Victor's death also illustrates how Roth plays with the circumstances of his own life in the series: his mother died of a sudden heart attack in 1981, the year *Zuckerman Unbound* was published, while his father would live for almost another decade. On his deathbed, Victor Zuckerman's last words are to call his oldest son, "Bastard" (193). The epithet unravels Nathan's sense of himself: the rebellious son who endeavored all his adult life "to leave little New Jersey and all the shallow provincials therein for the deep emancipating world of Art" now finds himself fatherless, his connection to his past broken, severed by both his father's disownment and death and how the 1967 riots have seemingly destroyed the Newark of his childhood.

Zuckerman's younger brother, Henry, makes an even more serious charge, suggesting that *Carnovsky* killed their father. "You killed him, Nathan," Henry accuses his brother. "Nobody will tell you—they're too frightened of you to say it. They think you're too famous to criticize—that you're far beyond the reach now of ordinary human beings. But you killed him, Nathan. With that book" (217). In a novel so interested in the unintended effects that a book can have on its readers, it seems only appropriate that Roth would add patricide to the possible outcomes that writing fiction might occasion. *Zuckerman Unbound* concludes with Zuckerman returning to Newark and his beloved Chancellor Avenue. The past, for Zuckerman, suddenly becomes much more substantial, more real, than the shabby and at times surreal existence in which he finds himself in the aftermath of his financial success and father's death. The novel ends when a "young black man" comes out of the house and asks who Zuckerman is, as his whiteness and wealth (he is being driven in a limousine) have made him conspicuous in his old neighborhood. "No one," Zuckerman responds (224). "You are no longer any man's son, you are no longer some good woman's husband, you are no longer your brother's brother, and you don't come from anywhere, either," Roth writes in the novel's final paragraph (224–5). Zuckerman's view appears incredibly narrow—he does little to think about the circumstances that triggered the riots that transformed Newark—but it does suggest how, in 1969, Zuckerman feels unmoored, his sense of himself completely collapsed. The writer who as a young man endeavored to rewrite his identity finds himself now disconnected from all the touchstones he used to define himself. Zuckerman's position could be seen as symptomatic of the state of the nation in 1969; his sense of having come undone seems like an appropriate response to the violence of those years.[13] Roth in *Zuckerman Unbound*, however, seems less interested in contextualizing the trauma of those years, but instead allows Zuckerman to wallow in his self-pity as the writer feels orphaned from all that has given his existence definition.

The sense of loss and the subsequent desire for renewal become the major themes of *The Anatomy Lesson* and *The Prague Orgy*, the final two volumes in the Zuckerman Bound sequence. *The Anatomy Lesson* opens with the now forty-year-old author addled by an undiagnosable pain in his neck and shoulders, unable to write, and grieving the death of his mother. Set in the final months of Richard Nixon's presidency, *The Anatomy Lesson* is the bleakest, but also the funniest, of the series as it chronicles Zuckerman's futile attempts to reinvent himself. The novel opens with a debilitated Zuckerman lying on a playmat in his Manhattan apartment, his head "supported by *Roget's Thesaurus*," and watching the Watergate hearings between visits from four women who serve his various sexual needs (10). "They were all the vibrant life he had," Roth writes of the women, "secretary-confidante-cook-housekeeper-companion—aside from the doses of Nixon's suffering, they were the entertainment. On his back he felt like their whore, paying in sex for someone to bring him the milk and the paper" (11–12). In its heightened focus on Zuckerman's physical pain, a pain that has no diagnosis and no moral, *The Anatomy Lesson* anticipates the emphasis on the declining body, an interest in rendering illness, that drives late works such as *Patrimony*, *The Dying Animal*, *Everyman*, and *Exit Ghost*.

Beyond this interest in the physical body, the novel captures Zuckerman's sense of belatedness as he finds himself disconnected from all the relationships that have formed his personal and creative identity. "Zuckerman had lost his subject," Roth writes in the opening of the second chapter. "His health, his hair, and his subject. Just as well he couldn't find a posture for writing. What he'd made his fiction from was gone—his birthplace the burnt-out landscape of a racial war and the people who'd been giants to him dead. . . . No new Newark was going to spring up again for Zuckerman, not like the first one: no fathers like those pioneering Jewish fathers bursting with taboos, no sons like their sons boiling with temptations, no loyalties, no ambitions, no rebellions, no capitulations, no clashes quite so convulsive again" (39–40). Zuckerman's view of Newark appears myopic at best: his views of the 1967 riot appear wholly informed by his childhood sense of the city as a sort of paradise that nurtured him. Indeed, it was not until *The Human Stain*, where Roth narrates Coleman Silk's perspective on growing up Black in nearby East Orange, New Jersey, that he seriously expanded his view of his childhood terrain to consider the African American experience. That said, Zuckerman's sense of disconnect from himself and his past has a certain resonance, reflecting the collective bewilderment and disillusionment that many Americans felt during the early 1970s as the Nixon presidency imploded and the Vietnam War wound down. The spectacle of Watergate looms over the novel; Roth even gives a minor character, a young novelist named Ivan Felt, the surname of the FBI agent, Mark Felt, who was long speculated to be Woodward and Bernstein's source in their investigation of Watergate, a rumor that was confirmed in 2005 when Felt, at the age of ninety-one, confessed to being the infamous Deep Throat.[14]

In the wake of the personal and national losses that he has experienced over the past decade, Zuckerman attempts to renew his life and his art. Zuckerman appears all too aware of the solipsistic nature of his fiction yet is unable to break free from the confines of thinking of himself; he simply lacks the energy to imagine other people. Listening to one of the women who frequent his apartment, Jaga, describe how she was raped by a taxi driver after leaving his apartment one night, Zuckerman wants to write her story, but finds himself unable: "Only what did he know? The story he could dominate and to which his feelings had been enslaved had ended. Her stories weren't his stories and his stories were no longer his stories either" (138). Lacking the energy to remake his fiction, Zuckerman turns to nursing old wounds. In the novel's most commented-upon section, Zuckerman has an explosive phone conversation with the literary critic Milton Appel, a figure clearly modeled on Irving Howe. As noted earlier, in 1972, Howe had published in *Commentary* his own devastating reappraisal of Roth's fiction, "Philip Roth Reconsidered," disparaging it as the product of a "thin personal culture."[15] The essay had particularly stung Roth because not only had Howe championed *Goodbye, Columbus*, but he also embodied the Jewish literary and intellectual life that Roth had so greatly admired at the start of his career. In his discussion of the ways in which he reimagined the Howe incident in *The Anatomy Lesson*, Roth commented, "There was the real autobiographical scene, and it had no life at all. I had to absorb the rage into the main character even if my own rage on this topic had long since subsided. By being true to life I was actually ducking the issue. So I reversed their positions, and had the twenty-year-old college girl [Diana] telling Zuckerman to grow up, and gave Zuckerman the tantrum. Much more fun" (*Why Write?* 161–2). The Howe/Appel episode in many ways best illustrates how Roth repurposes the events of his career and life for the Zuckerman novels, encouraging readers to accept the novels as straightforward autobiography while continually pulling the rug out from under such a reading.

Unable to write and incapacitated from pain, Zuckerman strives to return to the University of Chicago, where he studied literature twenty years earlier. Now, Zuckerman returns to Chicago to pursue medical school, an attempt to reclaim his identity as a good Jewish boy. On the flight to Chicago, Zuckerman, with an unhealthy mixture of alcohol and pain medicine in his system, professes to be Milton Appel, whom Zuckerman pretends is the proud publisher of a pornographic magazine, entitled *Lickety Split*. An intoxicated Nathan gleefully embodies the caricature of the crass pornographer that he has been accused of being, all the while privately besmirching the name of the moralizing critic who accused him of being debased. "Sex is changing in America," Zuckerman as Appel tells his seatmate on the plane, "people are swinging, eating pussy, women are fucking more, married men suck cocks, so *Lickety Split* reflects that. What are we supposed to do—lie? I see the statistics. These are real fundamental changes. As a revolutionary it's never enough for me" (182). It is a position that Roth will interrogate more seriously in *American Pastoral* where the academic Marcia Umanoff defends *Deep Throat* and gleefully laughs when Swede Levov's elderly father, Lou, is almost blinded by a fork wielded by a drunken dinner guest. However, in *The Anatomy Lesson*, Roth plays the position for a darkly comic laugh, as the disinhibited Zuckerman jubilantly becomes everything of which he has been accused. Not surprisingly, the trip does not end well for Zuckerman; he collapses in a Jewish graveyard, breaking his jaw on a gravestone. In the hospital, he takes one final impersonation—that of "resident humanist," indulging his fantasy of becoming a doctor of sorts. "For nearly as long as he remained a patient, Zuckerman roamed the busy corridors of the university hospital, patrolling and planning on his own by day," Roth writes in the novel's conclusion, "then out on the quiet floor with the interns at night, as though he still believed that he could unchain himself from a future as a man apart and escape the corpus that was his" (291).

The Prague Orgy brings the Zuckerman Bound series to a satisfying conclusion as Zuckerman appears to have pulled himself back together after the crises chronicled in *The Anatomy Lesson* and has resumed his literary life. The novella follows Zuckerman as he struggles once again to recover silenced Jewish voices—a manuscript of an unpublished Yiddish writer is at the center of the novella's plot, recalling *The Ghost Writer*'s endeavor to reclaim Anne Frank's voice. *The Prague Orgy* also brings history more to the forefront, a trend that will continue in the subsequent Zuckerman books, as Nathan grapples with the frightening realities that distort life and literature in the Eastern Bloc. Along with *The Professor of Desire* (1977), which features a section in Prague, *The Prague Orgy* would seem to be a result of Roth's work as the editor for Penguin's "Writers from the Other Europe" series, which had Roth making annual trips to Prague from 1973 until 1977, when he was denied an entry visa (*Why Write?* 413). "Prague," Ira Nadel writes, "became Roth's political unconscious, offering a more complex Jewish history than he could have ever known in Newark."[16] "When I was first in Czechoslovakia," Roth observed in 1984, "it occurred to me that I work in a society where as a writer everything goes and nothing matters, while for the Czech writers I met in Prague, nothing goes and everything matters. This isn't to say I wish to change places. I didn't envy them their persecution and the way in which it heightens their social importance. I didn't even envy them their seemingly more valuable and serious themes" (*Why Write?* 165).

Throughout *The Prague Orgy*, Zuckerman feels unsubstantial when compared to the oppressed writers he encounters in Czechoslovakia as he tries to recover the manuscripts of a never-published Yiddish writer, Sisovsky. The novella opens with Sisovsky's son, Zdenek, approaching Nathan in New York with a request: go to Prague to recover his father's fiction from Zdenek's estranged wife, Olga. Once in Prague, Zuckerman is brought to a party at the house of a Czech director, Klenek, where he is to meet Olga and begin his clandestine efforts to recover Sisovsky's manuscripts. "You like orgies," the writer Bolotka tells Nathan as an introduction to life in Prague, "you come with me. Since the Russians, the best orgies in Europe are in Czechoslovakia. Less liberty, better fucks. You can do whatever you want at Klenek's. No drugs, but plenty of whiskey. You can fuck, you can masturbate, you can look at dirty pictures, you can look at yourself in the mirror, you can do nothing. All the best people are there. Also the worst. We are all comrades now" (25). While the Zuckerman of *The Anatomy Lesson* might have leapt at Bolotka's invitation, he remains purposefully restrained. "They, silenced, are all mouth," Zuckerman says of his Czech colleagues. "I am only ears—and plans, an American gentleman abroad, with the bracing if old-fashioned illusion that he is playing a worthwhile, dignified, and honorable role" (37).

Zuckerman's attempt, however, to play an "honorable role" comes undone by *The Prague's Orgy*'s conclusion. Though he convinces a reluctant Olga to give him the lost manuscripts, he is stripped of them by the police while being interrogated by the Minister of Culture. "This is not the United States of America where every freakish thought is a fit subject for writing, where there is no such thing as propriety, decorum, or shame, nor a decent respect for the morality of the ordinary, hardworking citizen," the minister chides Zuckerman during his interrogation (81). Reminded of the realities of life in a totalitarian state, Zuckerman returns home without the manuscript, consigning another Jewish voice to remain lost to history. "Another assault upon a world of significance degenerating into a personal fiasco, and this time in a record forty-eight hours," Zuckerman proclaims at the end of the novella as he leaves Prague to return home to New York. "No, one's story isn't a skin to be shed—it's inescapable, one's body and blood. You go on pumping it out till you die, the story veined with the themes of your life, the ever-recurring story that's at once your invention and the invention of you" (84). At this moment, Zuckerman reconciles himself to his past and his sense of himself as a writer bound to that history. But more than this, Zuckerman's realization that your "story" is both "your invention and the invention of you" would seem to point the way forward for both Zuckerman and Roth. The necessity of fiction, the compulsive need to invent new stories, in constructing both personal identity and national history would be the idea that Roth would go on to explore in much of his later fiction. *The Prague Orgy*, then, is not a dead-end for Zuckerman, but instead marks the moment where Roth begins to expand his fiction, the novella's conclusion announcing the sense of creative renewal that would inform his fiction of the next decade.

This sense of renewal surfaces fully in *The Counterlife*. Published in 1986, *The Counterlife* remains one of Roth's most ambitious and successful novels; it won the National Book Critics Award for fiction in 1987, initiating the run of literary prizes and critical acclaim that Roth would enjoy for the next two decades. James Wood identified *The Counterlife* as "perhaps [Roth's] greatest novel," a work that "takes what it needs from postmodern self-consciousness and fictive games, and mounts a moving inquiry into what it means to lead a life."[17] Reflecting on his work after retiring from fiction writing, Roth affirmed *The Counterlife*'s importance in his career, describing it as the novel that "changed everything." "It was an aesthetic discovery, how to enlarge, how to amplify, how to be free," he observes in *Roth Unbound*.[18] Coming after the condensed Zuckerman Bound series, *The Counterlife* indeed feels expansive as Roth presents a sequence of five chapters that rebuke one another, a contradictory Pentateuch that explores the nexus of place, identity, and narrative. "This novel, to me, is a book of contradictory yet mutually entangling narratives," Roth observed in a 1986 interview. "I think the reader has the sensation from chapter to chapter of the rug being tugged from under him. . . . Zuckerman's English wife [Maria] pretty much sums things up when she says to him toward the end of the book, 'Radical change is the law of life,' and then adds, 'But you overdo it.'"[19]

Indeed, *The Counterlife* presents a series of "radical changes." In the novel's opening chapter, "Basel," Nathan's younger brother, Henry, dies in surgery meant to correct the impotence induced from a prior bypass surgery so that he can pursue his affair with his dental assistant; in the following section, "Judea," Henry is alive and well and has abandoned his family to emigrate to Israel; in the novel's fourth chapter it is Nathan who has died from heart surgery so that he can sleep with his upstairs neighbor, an Englishwoman named Maria (also the name that Zuckerman gives to Henry's first mistress, who had attempted to persuade Henry to move with her to Basel, Switzerland); and in the novel's final section, "Christendom," Zuckerman has been resurrected—although in the prior chapter we find out that we could be reading the manuscript that

Zuckerman was working on before dying—and is living in the English coun-
tryside with Maria, whom he has married and who is now pregnant with their
child. Reflecting on his brother's move to Israel, Zuckerman thinks, *"the kind
of stories that people turn life into, the kind of lives that people turn stories
into,"* a line that signals the novel's fascination with transformation and the
ways in which narrative remains a fundamental framework through which we
understand ourselves and the world in which we live (111). "Life *is* and," Zuckerman concludes in the novel's final section, "the accidental and the immutable,
the elusive and the graspable, the bizarre and the predictable, the actual and
the potential, all the multiplying realities, entangled, overlapping, colliding,
conjoined—plus the multiplying illusions! This times this times this times this
. . . Is an intelligent human being likely to be much more than a large-scale
manufacturer of misunderstanding?" (306). The novel would be simply dizzying if it were not so grounded in realism, each section displaying Roth's writing
at its most exact. The sections set in Israel—*The Counterlife* marks Roth's first
serious engagement with the Jewish homeland—and England are especially
impressive as they continue the engagement with the world outside of America
that Roth initiated with *The Prague Orgy*.

Beyond its playfulness, beyond the ways in which the book confounds readers' expectations for narrative cohesion, *The Counterlife* offers Roth's most
robust defense of the performative nature of identity while also positing his
critique of the pastoral, a critique that is essential to the historical questions
posed by the American Trilogy. At the end of the novel, Zuckerman tells his
pregnant wife Maria, who (through Zuckerman's own narrative invention) has
announced that she is leaving her husband's novel:

> All I can tell you with certainty is that I, for one, have no self, and that I am
> unwilling or unable to perpetrate upon myself the joke of a self. It certainly
> does strike me as a joke about *my* self. What I have instead is a variety of
> impersonations I can do, and not only of myself—a troupe of players that
> I have internalized, a permanent company of actors that I can call upon
> when a self is required, an ever-evolving stock of pieces and parts that forms
> my repertoire. But I certainly have no self independent of my imposturing,
> artistic efforts to have one. Nor would I want one. I am a theater and noth-
> ing more than a theater. (320–1)

Zuckerman's declaration that he is a "theater and nothing more" seems deeply
appropriate in a novel as interested in performance, in the ways our identities
shift when we inhabit a new place or encounter another person, as *The Counterlife* is. As Debra Shostak argues, Zuckerman's notion of the performative
self remains integral to the book's examination of Jewish identity: "For Roth,

this contradiction gets to the heart of the problem for the American Jew—as he wrote in the notes to the book in all caps, 'THERE IS NO SOLUTION TO THE JEWISH QUESTION.' In, particular, he inquiries into how an American can act—or be—authentically Jewish, given the fluidity of that category for the Diaspora Jew, whether the category is usefully delimited only by the geographical site that reverses the diasporic effect."[20] Beyond this, Zuckerman's assertion reflects Roth's fictive approach: how he inhabits different voices (Zuckerman, Alexander Portnoy, Mickey Sabbath, David Kepesh), tries on different positions, embraces the contradictory feelings and ideas that permeate our existence. *The Counterlife* captures Roth's insistence on multiplicity and contradiction, the endless and exhausting "ands" that constitute our attempts to understand ourselves and other people.

The Counterlife ends with Zuckerman embracing conflict and tension as the unifying elements of our existence. At the end of the novel, Zuckerman considers the desire for the pastoral, a quest for tranquility that would seem to negate the messy violence that constitutes existence: "Each has its own configuration, but whether set in the cratered moonscape of the Pentateuch, or the charming medieval byways of orderly old Schweiz, or the mists and the meadows of Constable's England, at the core is the idyllic scenario of redemption through the recovery of a sanitized, confusionless life" (322). Recognizing the desire for the pastoral within himself, seeing his desire to move to England and start a family with Maria as a product of his desire to free himself from his history, Zuckerman ends by embracing the Jewish ritual of circumcision: "Circumcision makes it clear as can be that you are here and not there, that you are out and not in—also that you're mine and not theirs. There is no way around it: you enter history through my history and me" (323). The insistence on violence, the impossibility of an existence free of strife and contradiction, remains central to the view of life that *The Counterlife* embraces, and one that Roth would go on to mine throughout the rest of his career.

Zuckerman would be resurrected as the narrator of the American Trilogy, but it would be more than twenty years before he would return as the central actor in one of Roth's novels. Published in 2007, *Exit Ghost* follows a seventy-year-old Zuckerman as he leaves his self-induced exile in the Berkshires and returns to Manhattan. Zuckerman is drawn out of seclusion by his infatuation with a much younger writer, Jamie Logan. The novel is a deliberate callback to *The Ghost Writer*, a connection hinted at in *Exit Ghost*'s title. It returns to the questions of literary production—how literary texts are produced and read—that Roth pursued in the first Zuckerman novel, but this time he explores them through an aging Zuckerman who is aware that he is losing his powers and worried about how his work will be read once he is dead. Perhaps not surprisingly, *Exit Ghost* remains the most difficult of Roth's late works; Nathan's memory loss can be felt throughout his narrative, and the novel as a whole reflects the intentional difficulty, the "sense of apartness and exile and anachronism" that Edward Said theorizes in his reading of late style.[21] A self-conscious exploration of aging's impact on the writer's imagination, *Exit Ghost* serves as a fitting end to the Zuckerman saga.

In New York, Zuckerman meets Richard Kliman, another younger writer, a friend of Jamie and her husband Billy, who aims to write a biography of E. I. Lonoff that promises to reveal an incestuous affair Lonoff had as a young man with his half-sister. Kliman's project outrages Zuckerman, and he promises to thwart its publication, his indignation driven less by the ways in which Lonoff's reputation might be besmirched than by how this revelation might flatten out the fiction, the purported incest threatening to become the primary lens through which future readers might comprehend Lonoff's work. Zuckerman also reencounters Amy Bellette, the woman he once fantasized was Anne Frank, and it is Bellette who voices the strongest objection to how literary culture has transformed (or devolved in her opinion) in the twenty-first century. Bellette's outrage is driven by Kliman's proposed biography and how the incest revelation will forever alter how Lonoff is read. "That will be the sum of Manny's achievement on earth—the sole fragment of him to be remembered," Bellette laments to Zuckerman. "To be *reviled*! Everything will be crushed beneath *that*" (196).

Bellette's indignation is balanced by Zuckerman's mourning of George Plimpton, the famous writer and founder of *The Paris Review*, who died in 2003. "George afforded my first glimpse of privilege and its vast rewards," Zuckerman recalls, "he seemingly had nothing to escape, no flaw to hide or injustice to defy or defect to compensate for or weakness to overcome or obstacle to circumvent, appearing instead to have learned everything and to be open to everything altogether effortlessly" (244). The "effortlessness" of Plimpton stands in stark contrast to Zuckerman and Roth's creative approach—Roth in interviews consistently emphasized the labor that writing fiction required. But beyond offering a contrast to Zuckerman's more strife-driven approach, Plimpton embodies a particular literary culture, one that has informed Roth's adult life. Plimpton's death, along with the deaths of Saul Bellow in 2005, Norman Mailer in 2007, and John Updike in 2009, would seem to signal the end of the culture that shaped Roth's life and career.

While it returns to the literary terrain covered in *The Ghost Writer*, *Exit Ghost* also offers a snapshot of American life in 2004, especially the political context of those years—George W. Bush's reelection is central to the novel's action, and Zuckerman's return to Manhattan is informed by the sense of loss triggered by the September 11th terrorist attacks on the World Trade Center. In contrast to Jamie Logan's outrage at Bush's reelection, Nathan remains slightly removed from the trauma of the election. "I thought to repeat, It's amazing how much punishment we can take," Zuckerman thinks of what he wants to tell Jamie as Bush's victory over John Kerry is confirmed. "I thought to say, If in America you think like you do, nine times out of ten you fail. I thought to say, It's bad, but not like waking up the morning after Kennedy was shot. It's bad, but not like waking up the morning after Martin Luther King was shot. It's bad, but not like waking up the morning after the Kent States students were shot. I thought to say, We have all been through it. But I said nothing" (86). On the one hand, Zuckerman here appears to be very much the product of his own historical circumstances, privileging the historical trauma that has shaped his sense of his nation as a young adult. Yet, there is a broader lesson here too: a contextualization of Bush's victory and his misbegotten War on Terror as another trauma in the countless violent disturbances that constitute American history.

The novel ends, however, with Zuckerman's final literary production, a short play entitled *He and She*, a play that rewrites his infatuation with the happily married Logan. "But isn't one's pain quotient shocking enough without fictional amplification, without giving things an intensity that is ephemeral in life and sometimes even unseen? Not for some," Zuckerman says of the impetus behind the play. "For some very, very few that amplification, evolving uncertainly out of nothing, constitutes their only assurance, and the unlived, the surmise, fully drawn in print on paper, is the life whose meaning comes to matter most" (147). Zuckerman's admission here captures how narrative, spinning stories out of the raw materials of life, becomes the primary way in which he understands his life, the fiction enabling him to relish in the agony of his unrequited sexual desire. The play, a fragment of just two voices, also becomes a reflection of Zuckerman's diminished self. Unable to work up the energy to create a full narrative as he had as a young man for Amy Bellette/ Anne Frank in *The Ghost Writer*, Zuckerman can only create the voices themselves. The play and the novel end with the "She" voice agreeing to come over for a sexual encounter, a reversal of their platonic relationship. In the play's final moment, Zuckerman leaves before Jamie can arrive to consummate their relationship. "*He disintegrates*," Roth, as Zuckerman, writes in the stage directions that conclude the novel. "*She's on her way and he leaves. Gone for good*" (292). The ending, with Zuckerman evaporating into thin air, remains a wholly appropriate ending for Roth's most famous alter-ego. A character who began his existence as the fictional creation of one of Roth's other characters, Peter Tarnopol, simply disappears from his own story. As Roth approached the end of his career, it seems only right that he would give Zuckerman a sort of immortality, allowing him to escape the inevitability (and permanence) of death and to disappear into the ether of his own fictional narrative.

CHAPTER 4

Sex and the Serious Life
The Kepesh Trilogy

Starting with *The Breast* (1972), Roth chronicled the sexual and literary education of David Kepesh, the literature professor who would star in two subsequent Roth novels, *The Professor of Desire* (1977) and *The Dying Animal*
(2001). The Kepesh trilogy, in many respects, remains a minor component of
Roth's oeuvre—the three books lack the narrative ambition that characterizes
much of his most successful fiction—yet in their dealing with the frequently unsettling nature of male sexuality, how the pursuit of sex can derail a man's sense
of himself and his relationships with others, the books seem to be quintessen-
tial Roth. Surveying the notions of masculinity that emerge in Roth's fiction,
Debra Shostak discerns that "Roth's interest in the lives of twentieth-century
American men has often taken shape in narratives of heterosexual pursuit. . . .
Roth has seemed not just to risk but even to welcome censure; at times he has
written male characters as if simply to learn what they will do and whether
there are reasons not to despise them."[1] Indeed, the Kepesh books could easily
be used as evidence to support the charge of misogyny that has frequently been
leveled against Roth; Kepesh certainly objectifies women, and his views of sex
can be retrograde and unsettling. "The decades since the sixties have done a
remarkable job of completing the sexual revolution," Kepesh observes early in
The Dying Animal in a moment that is characteristic of his view of sex. "This
is a generation of astonishing fellators. There's been nothing like them ever
before among their class of young women" (8–9). While passages like this have
been cited by critics who have dismissed Roth as an avowed misogynist, such
a reading mistakenly assumes Kepesh to be a straightforward mouthpiece for
Roth's own views on women and sex, a type of misreading, to be fair, that his

fiction often invites—this is a writer after all who has employed a fictional version of himself as the protagonist of several of his books.[2]

Such readings, however, miss the ways that Roth interrogates, and even
undermines, Kepesh's views on women and sex through the course of the trilogy. In one of his final interviews, Roth remarked that he was "no stranger as a
novelist to the erotic furies." "I haven't shunned the hard facts in these fictions
of why and how and when tumescent men do what they do, even when these
have not been in harmony with the portrayal that a masculine public-relations
campaign—if there were such a thing—might prefer," Roth elaborated. "I've
stepped not just inside the male head but into the reality of those urges whose
obstinate pressure by its persistence can menace one's rationality, urges sometimes so intense they may even be experienced as a form of lunacy."[3] Indeed, the
trilogy persists as Roth's most concentrated and unflinching exploration of the
"male head," the books chronicling how Kepesh, despite his education, remains
trapped by his sexual desires. While chronicling the contradictions of male sexuality has been one of Roth's primary concerns as a novelist, the Kepesh series,
especially *The Breast* and *The Professor of Desire*, have received relatively little
critical attention, and the trilogy as whole has frequently been relegated to the
outskirts of Roth's oeuvre. Mike Witcombe observes that Kepesh remains "the
least narratively coherent of Roth's recurrent narrators" and stands as "one
of Roth's most enigmatic characters."[4] The trilogy's final volume, *The Dying
Animal*, largely ignores the backstory established in the earlier novels: Kepesh
would seem to have no memory of his time spent as a female breast—nor does
Roth ever explain how the good professor escaped this predicament—and his
description of his first wife bears little resemblance to the character of Helen
Baird whom Kepesh impulsively marries in *The Professor of Desire*. In *The Dying Animal*, Roth even gives Kepesh an indignant adult son, Kenny, who does
not exist in the prior two books.

Adding to the difficulty of the series is the fact that the three books are
written in very different modes—the surrealism of *The Breast*, the more conventional realism of *The Professor of Desire*, and the unnamed (and unspeak-
ing) conversational partner who stands behind *The Dying Animal*—and these
changes in narrative approach make the Kepesh series one of Roth's most
challenging reads. Such narrative inconsistencies make for occasionally difficult
reading, but they signal how Roth ultimately uses the character as a sort of
receptacle through which he can interrogate certain notions of male sexuality and the human body. Despite their scattershot approach, the three books
remain central to Roth's fictive project, as they constitute his most sustained
inquiry into the intersections between art, sex, and gender politics. The Kepesh
books are both a reflection of the sexual politics that informed their time—*The*

Breast capitalizes on the shifting sexual mores that helped make *Portnoy's Complaint* a bestseller—and a reflection on how attitudes toward sex changed radically during Roth's lifetime. In a 2001 interview that followed *The Dying Animal*'s publication, Roth observed that the "three Kepesh books depict three alternative erotic lives—think of the trilogy as a sequence of dreams, here and there at variance with one another in the manner of dreams but essentially putting the same intelligent and rational hero through his life's self-defining ordeal: having to think his way through a sizable sexual predicament laden with contradiction and incongruities."[5] Read as dream sequence, as a series of texts that play off one another rather than narrate a stable history, the trilogy's importance to Roth's fictive project becomes more readily apparent, the three slim books offering an unsettling history of American sexual life in the second half of the twentieth century. As a cultural critic, Kepesh remains limited by his own prejudices and predilections—Roth frequently undercuts Kepesh's vehement advocacy for sexual freedom over the course of the three novels— yet his perspective offers a complicated lens through which Roth exposes the consequences of Kepesh's sexual drives while also illuminating the culture that helped shape those desires.

Published in 1972, only three years after the commercial and critical success of *Portnoy's Complaint*, *The Breast* amplifies the comic absurdity that charac- terized that novel as well as *Our Gang*. Chronicling David Kepesh's inexplicable transformation into a six-foot female mammary, *The Breast* is the strang- est entry in the Kepesh series—Roth never explains what triggers Kepesh's transformation—and remains Roth's most inscrutable book. The novella can perhaps be best understood as part of Roth's attempts to redefine himself as a writer, a refashioning that began with *Portnoy's Complaint* and that continued throughout the early 1970s. "The direction my work has taken since *Portnoy's Complaint* can in part be accounted for by my increased responsiveness to, and respect for, what is unsocialized in me," Roth observed in a 1973 self-interview. "I don't mean that I am interested in propagandizing for the anarcho-libidinists in our midst; rather, *Portnoy's Complaint*, which was concerned with the comic side of the struggle between a hectoring superego and an ambitious id, seems now, in retrospect, to have realigned those forces as they act upon my imagina- tion" (*Reading Myself* 76–7). Forgoing the Jamesian seriousness that defined his early fiction, Roth transformed himself into a comedic performer in these mid-career books—the novels following *Portnoy's* were the most outlandish (and uneven) books he would ever produce as he attempted to surpass the riotous comic spirit he had unleashed in that novel. Perhaps not surprisingly, *The Breast* offers an oblique reflection on the fame and notoriety that Roth gained after *Portnoy's Complaint*, with Kepesh lamenting that he has become a spectacle for a curious public to consume. "For all I know," Kepesh speculates early in the novella, "I may be under a soundproof dome on a platform in the middle of Madison Square Garden, or in Macy's window—and what difference would it make?" (19).[6]

In its original incarnation—Roth republished the novella in 1980 and 1989 with small stylistic adjustments—*The Breast* is an especially performative (and verbose) text as Kepesh attempts to articulate what has happened to him. "I know about the perspective from which everything appears awesome and mysterious," Kepesh announces in the book's opening paragraph. "Reflect upon eternity, consider, if you are up to it, oblivion, and everything that is is a wonder. Still and all I would submit to you, in all humility, that some things are more wonderous than others, and I am one such thing" (3). The difficulty of the syntax here reflects Kepesh's voice throughout *The Breast*, one shaped by the intellectual posturing that he has internalized as an academic. Witcombe points out that Roth revised Kepesh's style in the 1980 and the 1989 editions of the novel to make the prose "more fluid" but in doing so he "undermine[d] the thematic significance of Kepesh's self-indulgent prose."[7] In the 1972 version, Kepesh's performativity is especially evident as he uses language to help comprehend his transformation, a change that resists any medical (or moral) explanation. Kepesh's narrative swerves wildly between his attempts to rationalize or parse his transformation and his ever-escalating sexual fantasies, which are a byproduct of the physical sensations he now feels as a giant female breast with a seven-inch nipple. "*You* want me to be *ordinary*—*you* expect me to be *ordinary* in this condition," Kepesh exclaims to his psychiatrist, Dr. Klinger, in an extended rant where he laments his girlfriend Claire's refusal to have sex with him in his new condition. "I'm supposed to be a sensible man—when I am like this! But that's crazy on your part, Doctor! I want [Claire] to sit on me with her cunt! Why not! I want Claire to! *Why won't Claire do it!* She'll do everything else! Why won't she do that! Why is that too grotesque!" (36).

Despite their comedic potential, these outbursts devolve into something sadder, and *The Breast* remains a largely melancholy chronicle of Kepesh's attempts to compensate for the loss of his physical existence as a man. Responding to the notion that *The Breast* possessed an "elegiac tone," Roth commented, "I'm not sure I'd call the tone elegiac. It's a sad story and Kepesh is mournful sometimes, but it's more to the point to say that there is an elegiac note *trying* to make itself heard but held in check by the overriding (and, I think, in the circumstances, ironic) tone of reasonableness. The mood is less plaintive than reflective—the horror recollected in a kind of stunned tranquility. The mood of the convalescent" (*Reading Myself* 73–4). As Roth's remarks here suggest, *The Breast* is not so much an outlandish comedy as it is a serious, albeit bizarre, consideration of the connection between subjectivity and the physical body; despite his transformation, David Kepesh's sense of himself as a man and as an intellectual remains constant, the novel tracing how the professor struggles to reconcile his sense of himself with his transformation into an explicitly female body part, one that has been frequently objectified and fetishized. Throughout *The Breast*, Kepesh appears deeply aware of the ways he is being viewed—he is mortified when his department chair, Arthur Schonbrunn, visits and is unable to contain his laughter—and his pangs of sexual desire, his desperate need for his girlfriend to insert his nipple into her, can be viewed as a clear overcompensation for having lost his identity as a man.

The novella concludes with Kepesh not rethinking his notion of masculinity, but instead embracing an image of himself as sexual celebrity, an object to be ravished by "twelve- and thirteen-year-old girls" (74). "If the Rolling Stones can find them, if Charles Manson can find them, we can find them," Kepesh tells Dr. Klinger at the end of the book. "There will also be women who will want to open their thighs to something as new and thrilling as my nipple" (75). Kepesh's performance here is deeply ironic; he is both lampooning the absurdity of his situation while failing to move beyond the strictures of masculinity and sexuality that seem deeply ingrained within him. He concludes by comparing himself to "Gulliver among the Brobdingnags," recalling the episode in Swift's novel where the "king's maidservants had the befuddled Gulliver 'walk out on their nipples for the fun of it'" (75). Kepesh somewhat desperately positions himself as a figure of the Sexual Revolution: "but this, my friend, is the Land of Opportunity in the Age of Self-Fulfillment, and I am David Alan Kepesh, the Breast, and I will live by my own lights!" (75). Here he clings to both his identity as a man and a breast, one who might take advantage of the shifting sexual mores of the early 1970s—the emphasis on self-fulfillment and sexual freedom—that he was too cautious to engage in when he was a respectable English professor. If he has lost his desire for sex as a man—the book opens with Kepesh recalling how his relationship with Claire had been largely sexless in the period before he began to feel the effects of his transformation—Kepesh's libido and his ability to articulate his desires appear rejuvenated in his new state—the transformation disinhibiting him and allowing him to express the sexual urges that he has previously attempted to contain.

The directness of Kepesh's sexual desire at the end of the novella—he fantasizes that he will have "three, four, five, six" girls "naked and giggling, stroking and sucking me for days on end" (75)—stands in stark contrast to the remainder of his narration as he struggles to analyze his bizarre predicament, to read it as if it were a literary text that could be broken open if only studied closely enough. On the one hand, *The Breast* can be read as narrative about the

limits of literature as a way of comprehending oneself or the outer world, as
Kepesh's comparison to *Gulliver's Travels* suggests. At one point, he playfully
suggests that he perhaps taught Kafka's "The Metamorphosis" and Gogol's
"The Nose" with too much "conviction" (55). Rejecting any simple moral behind his transformation, Kepesh professes, "Reality is grander than [the simple
moralizing of fairy tales]. Reality has more style. There. For those of you who
cannot live without one, a moral to this tale. 'Reality has style,' concludes the
embittered professor who became a female breast" (34). Literature, as way
of understanding the world, has its limits, and reality remains more fantastic
and absurd than the most outlandish fiction, a lesson that Roth would return
to more seriously in *American Pastoral* and *The Plot Against America*. "To
try and unravel the mystery of 'meaning' here is really to participate to some
degree in Kepesh's struggle—and to be defeated, as he is," Roth explained in
a 1972 interview. "Not all the ingenuity of all the English teachers in all the
English departments in America can put David Kepesh together again. For him
there is no way out of the monstrous situation, not even through literary inter-
pretation" (*Reading Myself* 69). Kepesh's training as a scholar—his ability to
produce clever interpretations of a novel, to uncover its covert meanings—fails
him when he encounters the inexplicable and the meaningless.

Roth more fully explores the consequences of a life devoted to literature in
The Professor of Desire, a prequel of sorts to *The Breast*. Published five years
after *The Breast*, *The Professor of Desire* chronicles Kepesh's life before turning
into a breast: his picturesque childhood in the Catskills resort his parents run;
his first attempts at sex as an undergraduate when he pitifully cajoles a cheer-
leader into letting him kiss her belly ("No higher and no lower," she instructs
him) [26]; his experience abroad in England as a Fulbright scholar where he
enjoys his newfound sexual freedom with two Swedish girls; a disastrous first
marriage to Helen Baird, a more comic version of the Maureen Tarnopol character in *My Life as a Man*; and finally his relationship with Claire Ovington, a
devoted teacher and staid lover who is Kepesh's romantic partner in *The Breast*.
The novel largely centers on Kepesh's struggles to reconcile the domestic peace
that he finds in his relationship with Claire with his longing for the invigorating
sexual life that they enjoyed when first dating. Written in the first person and
the present tense, *The Professor of Desire* lacks the verbal fireworks that are on
display in *The Breast*, and the book stands as one of Roth's breeziest and even
most sentimental works. Coming after the inventive but exhaustive *My Life as
A Man*, *The Professor of Desire* marks a vital moment of transition for Roth
as he was moving away from the comic extremes that had characterized his
output since *Portnoy's Complaint*. Assessing the novel's place in Roth's oeuvre,
Claudia Roth Pierpont reflects that it "mixes outgrown themes with energetic,

imaginatively charged new signs and scenes, and with a muted tenderness that is like nothing in his work before. It is neither a book one would want to be without nor a fulfilled achievement."[8]

Pierpont's assessment here resonates, suggesting how *The Professor of Desire* anticipates the more deeply felt work that Roth would produce in the following decade, in particular the Zuckerman Bound series. The novel contains segments and ideas that Roth would develop more fully in his later fiction. In a minor episode, Kepesh recalls his college roommate, Louis Jelinek, a homosexual and masturbation fiend. Jelinek, whose obnoxious behavior both repels and attracts Kepesh, would seem to be a comic inversion of the doomed Marcus Messner in Roth's 2009 novel, *Indignation*. Like Messner, Jelinek gets himself expelled from his university, but instead of letting himself get shipped off to Korea, Jelinek goes AWOL from the Army during the Korean War, leading to an FBI investigation. "And after he leaves I am appalled by the way I have conducted myself: my terror of prison, my Lord Fauntleroy manners, my collaborationist instincts—and my shame over just about everything," Kepesh recounts of his encounter with the FBI agent investigating his expelled roommate's disappearance (22).

Beyond the way it anticipates Roth's later work, *The Professor of Desire* marks Roth's most sustained interrogation of the values and the context that shaped his generation's intellectual and sexual sensibilities. As his encounter with the FBI agent demonstrates, Kepesh, despite his attempts to rebel, remains very much a product of the conformist and conservative sexual politics of the 1950s: he frets that the FBI agent believes he is gay and quickly, to his horror, folds to the social and political expectations of the early Cold War that prioritized appearances and conformity. The first sections of the novel—where Kepesh recounts his college experience and then his time abroad in London where he falls into a torrid sexual affair with two Swedish students, Elisabeth and Birgitta—further reflect the sexual norms that Kepesh internalized in his youth and help illuminate the sexual ideas that account for his self-image in *The Breast*. "Given the reputation, you would think that I had already reduced a hundred coeds to whoredom, when in fact in four years' time I actually succeeded in achieving full penetration on but two occasions, and something vaguely resembling penetration on two more," Kepesh says of his college sexual experience (23).

The carefulness with which he delineates his different sexual encounters—his meticulous mentioning of the women he has almost penetrated—illustrates the extent to which he remains tethered to the sexual expectations of his era, expectations that also informed Roth's own views of sex as a young man. Recalling his first serious college girlfriend in *The Facts*, Roth describes how he pestered her for sex, "the independent, no-nonsense wit who for months treated my declarations of feeling and my sexual persistence as an incomprehensible nuisance" (70). Such sexual attitudes inform many of Roth's male protagonists—Alex Portnoy approaches sex from a similar vantage point, and Marcus Messner in *Indignation* cannot comprehend that his college girlfriend would voluntarily give him oral sex—but Roth most acutely demonstrates their destabilizing consequences in the character of David Kepesh, who struggles to reconcile his sexual desire with his notion of the respectable life he feels like he should lead (a respectability that is, of course, shattered when he transforms into a breast). "Why did I like you so much," his Swedish girlfriend, the sexually adventurous Birgitta, asks when Kepesh breaks off their relationship. "You are such a boy" (50). It's a charge that sticks; despite his graduate education, Kepesh appears stunted throughout the novel as he struggles to understand his relationship with women and his own sexual desires.

The study of literature would seem to be a corrective force for Kepesh, the writers he studies (Flaubert, Chekhov, Kafka) offering him a way of understanding, and perhaps refining, the tumult—the sense of conflict and desire for more—that he sees as essential to the erotic life. Nevertheless, his attempts to imagine the study of literature—after his time as a Fulbright he pursues a Ph.D. in comparative literature—as a reprieve from the complications brought on by sex are undermined throughout the novel. "I hate libraries, I hate books, and I hate schools," Helen Baird tells her future husband early in their courtship. "As I remember, they tend to turn everything about life into something slightly other than it is—'slightly' at best. It's those poor innocent theoretical bookworms who do the teaching who turn it all into something worse" (59–60). While Helen remains a somewhat preposterous character—she spends her twenties as something of a sexual adventurer in Hong Kong, where she finds herself embroiled in an affair with a rich, older man who later threatens to kill her—her critique of literature resonates, suggesting that novels do not simply reflect reality or imbue it with meaning and order, but instead alter life, "slightly" distorting it. It is a lesson Kepesh struggles to learn as he continues to use literature as way of imagining life. Midway through the novel, he contemplates teaching a course on literature and desire where he would confess his own erotic history alongside the novels of "Tolstoy, Mann, and Flaubert" (184). "To put it as straight as I can," Kepesh declares near the conclusion of the imagined opening lecture, "what a church is to the true believer, a classroom is to me. Some kneel at Sunday prayer, others don phylacteries each dawn . . . and I appear three times each week, my tie around my neck and my watch on my desk, to teach the great stories to you" (185). While the speech that Kepesh composes is playful, a comic riff on Franz Kafka's short story "A Report to an Academy," in which an ape speaks to a scientific gathering, the faith that Kepesh places in literature and in the classroom is serious, suggesting the ways in which he believes in literature's capacity for transforming the confusion of sex and desire, for giving it shape and meaning.

The novel's consideration of the literary, however, reaches its apex in its midsection when Kepesh visits Prague, where Roth traveled regularly between 1973 and 1977 as the editor of Penguin's "Writers from the Other Europe" series. In Prague, Kepesh and Claire visit the Kafka sites, including the writer's carefully tended grave where "the family-haunted-son is buried—still!—between the mother and the father who outlived him" (175). The scene unexpectedly fosters a sense of domestic contentment within Kepesh, and he notes that he feels "overwhelmingly in love" with his partner as "I pick Claire's clothes off the bed and pack them in her suitcase" (179). The sentimentality of that evening and the notions of love inspired by the visit to Kafka's grave are undercut by a dream Kepesh has that night where he visits a prostitute, Eva, who claims to have serviced Kafka as a young man. The sequence, which anticipates Nathan Zuckerman's fantasies regarding Anne Frank in *The Ghost Writer*, is the most outrageous (and funny) moment within the novel as Roth skewers the literary tourist industry and the dynamics that surround Eastern bloc writers and their Western advocates. "First of all, given your field of interest, the money is tax-deductible," Kepesh's guide informs him as he persuades Kepesh to pay five dollars to inspect Eva's vagina. "Second, for only a fiver, you are striking a decisive blow against the Bolsheviks. She is one of the last in Prague still in business for herself. Third, you are helping preserve a national literary monument—you are doing a service for our suffering writers" (192).

The novel's concluding section moves away from the outlandishness of Kepesh's dream—where he ends up paying the money to examine the woman that Kafka purportedly used for sex—to exploring Kepesh's newfound domestic happiness with Claire, a happiness that he doubts can be sustained, and his reconciliation with his father. As Mark Shechner concludes, *"The Professor of Desire* is Roth's tenderest book, the one in which he takes the greatest risks of love. It dispenses almost entirely with irony, crisis, compulsion, moral intricacy, and the comic strategies of self-defeat, and attempts to make a simple statement of the power of nurturance to heal what is broken in life."[9] In the concluding section, Kepesh's father and an elderly Holocaust survivor, Mr. Barbatnik, visit Kepesh and Claire in their newfound domestic tranquility. One night, Barbatnik shares his experience during the Second World War and how he survived the unimaginable: first the violence of the Holocaust and then the death of his second wife, also a survivor of the Holocaust, from brain cancer. "And it happened out of nowhere," Barbatnik says of his second wife's death, a line that suggests the ways in which the unpredictability of life will come to the forefront in Roth's late fiction (258). After a dinner together, Kepesh reflects on the evening, comparing it to a "Chekhov story":

> This. Today. The summer. Some nine or ten pages, that's all. Called 'The Life I Formerly Led.' Two old men come to the country to visit a healthy, handsome young couple, brimming over with contentment. The young man is in his middle thirties, having recovered finally from the mistakes of his twenties. The young woman is in her twenties, the survivor of a painful youth and adolescence. They have every reason to believe they have come through. It looks and feels to both of them as though they have been saved, and in large part by one another. They are in love. But after dinner by candlelight, one of the other old men tells of his life, and about the blows that keep on coming. And that's it. The story ends just like this: her pretty head on his shoulder; his hand stroking her hair; their owl hooting; their constellations all in order—their medallions all in order; their guests in their freshly made beds; and their summer cottage so cozy and inviting, just down the hill from where they sit together wondering about what they have to fear. Music is playing in the house. The most lovely music there is. 'And both of them knew that that the most complicated and difficult part was only just beginning.' That's the last line of [Chekhov's] 'Lady with a Lapdog.' (259–60)

Kepesh's reverie suggests he still relies on literature as a reference for understanding his life—Chekhov's language giving shape and a sense of grace to the most unsettling of feelings. Kepesh realizes that the sense of contentment he feels at this moment will not last; like many of Roth's protagonists, Kepesh longs for the peace promised by the pastoral while also realizing that such promises are ultimately unsustainable. Roth's novel, however, doesn't end with the pastoral tranquility of a Chekhov story, but instead with the image of Kepesh desperately sucking at Claire's breast. It's a conclusion that not only cleverly foreshadows his impending transformation, but also illustrates that such tranquility, for Roth's male protagonists, will always be short-lived. The chaos of life, "the blows that keep on coming," as well as the tumult of the sexual impulse, will always persist. "But even while I suck in a desperate frenzy at the choicest morsel of her flesh," Kepesh laments in the novel's concluding sentence, "even as I pit my accumulated happiness, and all my hope, against my fear of transformations yet to come, I wait to hear the most dreadful sound imaginable emerge from the room where Mr. Barbatnik and my father lie alone and insensate, each in his freshly made bed" (263). The happiness that Kepesh experiences in *The Professor of Desire* appears even more poignant for how transient is, Kepesh's sucking at Claire's breasts revealing how desperately he clings to this domestic peace, this sense of emotional renewal and repleteness, while it lasts.

After nearly a quarter century hiatus, Roth returned to the character of Kepesh in *The Dying Animal,* the final and richest entry in the trilogy. Eschewing the frenetic comic antics that characterized the first two books, *The Dying Animal* offers an unsettling meditation on aging, male sexuality, and the end of the "American century." "Can you imagine old age," Kepesh asks early in his narrative, a question that reverberates through much of the fiction that Roth would produce during the last decade of his career. "Of course you can't. I didn't. I couldn't. I had no idea what it was like. Not even a false image—no image. And nobody wants anything else. Nobody wants to face any of this before he has to" (35). The novel also commemorates the end of the "American century," as Kepesh watches the televised New Year celebrations marking the new millennium. "No bombs go off, no blood is shed—the next bang you hear will be the boom of prosperity and the explosion of markets," Kepesh muses of the televised New Year celebrations. "The slightest lucidity about the misery made ordinary by our era sedated by the grandiose illusion" (145). In its brevity, the novel stands as a precursor to the short, death-obsessed books that Roth would produce at the very end of his career while also providing a disquieting conclusion to the trilogy. Taking the form of a conversation between Kepesh and a silent unnamed interlocutor, the novel traces Kepesh's ruminations on Consuela Castillo, a much younger Cuban American former student with whom he pursued a relatively brief sexual affair. Their affair began as one of the flings that Kepesh embarks on annually—he acknowledges early in the novel that his one rule as a professor has been not to pursue a sexual relationship with a student until her final grades have been submitted "so as not to run afoul of those in the university, who, if they could, would seriously impede my enjoyment of life" (5).

His relationship with Consuela, however, transforms into something more substantial and disturbing when she returns years later to announce that, at the age of thirty-two, she has been diagnosed with breast cancer and that she has elected to have a double mastectomy. Kepesh links the narrative of Consuela's illness with the demise of his friend George O'Hearn, a poet and fellow raconteur who suffers a devastating stroke and dies at the age of fifty-five. The novel's peculiar form—Roth never reveals who Kepesh is talking to, and the other voice never speaks until the book's closing lines—amplifies its impact, as Kepesh struggles to comprehend the effect these illnesses have on his sense of himself and the encroaching nearness of death. "What's so hilarious? My didacticism," Kepesh asks midway through the book. "I agree:

one's absurd side is never unimpressive. But what can be done about it? I'm a critic, I'm a teacher—didacticism is my destiny. Argument and counterargument is what history's made of. One either imposes one's idea or is imposed on" (112). Kepesh's acknowledgement of his method could be applied to Roth more broadly—in many ways, his novels can be read as a relentless series of arguments and counterarguments—but *The Dying Animal* unsettles Kepesh's arguments, revealing he now struggles to believe the views on sex and freedom that he loudly professes.

If the first two books in the trilogy dissect Kepesh's sense of himself as a sexual creature—the way his masculinity remains intertwined with his libido —*The Dying Animal* captures how Kepesh is undone by sex, his desire for Consuela and the consequences of breast cancer on her body unmooring the emotionally stunted Kepesh. *The Dying Animal*, ultimately, is not so much a celebration of Kepesh's sexual freedom, but instead a problematic meditation on the actual costs of that freedom. Published in the immediate wake of the critical success of the American Trilogy, *The Dying Animal* pursues many of the historical questions that haunt novels such as *American Pastoral* and *The Human Stain* as the now sixty-year-old Kepesh surveys his life, particularly how the sexual rebellions of the 1960s shaped his worldview: "But I was determined, once I saw the disorder for what it was, to seize from the moment a rationale for myself, to undo my former allegiances, not to be, as many my age were, either inferior to it or superior to it or simply titillated by it, but to follow the logic of this revolution to its conclusion, and without having become its casualty" (62–3).

Roth largely jettisons the history that he gave Kepesh in *The Breast* and *The Professor of Desire*, and instead positions him as a witness to and participant in the sexual changes that reshaped American life during the late 1960s and early 1970s. Mulling the impact of those years, Kepesh recalls two of his former students, Carolyn Lyons and Janie Wyatt, who, "along with another three or four defiant upper-middle-class kids, comprised a clique calling itself the Gutter Girls" (60). The Gutter Girls were "Abbie Hoffman"-esque sexual radicals whose forthright sexuality and sexual antics exploded campus life during the late 1960s, much as the Weather Underground had bombed buildings. "The blow job in the library is the very essence of it, the sanctified transgression, the campus black mass," Janie Wyatt declares in her senior thesis, "A Hundred Ways to be Perverse in the Library," confirming how the Gutter Girls embraced the performativity of the era, transferring the tactics of political theater to the bedroom and the classroom (48). "They and their adherents may well have been, historically, the first wave of American girls fully implicated in their own desire," Kepesh muses in his professorial manner. "No rhetoric, no ideology, just the playing field of pleasure opening out to the bold. The boldness developed as they realized what the possibilities were, when they realized they were no longer being watched, that they were no longer subservient to the old system or under any system of any kind—when the realized they could do anything" (50–1).

Perhaps not surprisingly, Kepesh celebrates the changes that women like the Gutter Girls triggered, not only for the ways women like Janie and Carolyn were able to assert their sexual agency, but also for how their revolution helped liberate him from the sexual constraints he had felt as a young man. Although a generation removed from Janie and Carolyn, Kepesh was more than happy to partake in the sexual opportunities they provided, a new sexual openness that led to the end of his first marriage. (Incidentally, this marriage would seem to bear no resemblance to Kepesh's union with Helen Baird in *The Professor of Desire*). "Having those girls in class was my education," Kepesh concludes of his experience with the Gutter Girls, "seeing how they got themselves up, watching them jettison their manners and uncover their crudeness, listening to their music with them, smoking with them and listening to Janis Joplin, their Bessie Smith in whiteface, their shouter, their honky-tonk, stoned Judy Garland" (56). Kepesh does not see them as an anomaly, but instead positions their sexual theatrics within a forgotten strain of American life that can be traced back to the Plymouth Puritans and the figure of Thomas Morton, a British-born lawyer and raconteur who oversaw an infamous seventeenth-century trading post at Merry Mount, a location that (as Kepesh notes) Nathaniel Hawthorne would later immortalize in his short story, "The May-Pole of Merry Mount" (1832). "The Puritans were terrified that their daughters would be carried off and corrupted by this merry miscegnator out at Merry Mount," Kepesh writes of Morton. "A white man, a white Indian, luring the virgins away? This was even more sinister than red Indians stealing them away. Morton was going to turn their daughters into the Gutter Girls" (59). Kepesh's description of an America divided between its Puritan legacy and that legacy's counter—the sexualized freedom embodied by Morton—remains characteristic of Roth's historical vision of how America's obsession with purity is always threatened by its more chaotic reality. "No, the sixties weren't aberrant," Kepesh concludes. "The Wyatt girl wasn't aberrant. She was a natural Mortonian in the conflict that's been ongoing from the beginning. Out in the American wildness, order will reign. The Puritans were the agents of rule and godly virtue and right reason, and on the other side was misrule. Why isn't Morton the great theologian of no-rules? Why isn't Morton seen for what he is, the founding father of personal freedom?" (61).

Kepesh's arguments for the importance of Morton's legacy, his advocacy for the primacy of "personal freedom," is undercut by the consequences that his sexual behavior triggers, a critique forcefully articulated by Kepesh's adult son, Kenny. The embittered son of Kepesh's first marriage, Kenny counters his father's advocacy for sexual freedom and liberated manhood. At the age of forty-two, a married father, Kenny blames his father for abandoning him and his mother during his childhood—he is the collateral damage of Kepesh's encounter with the Gutter Girls—while also seeking Kepesh's advice as he finds himself embroiled in an affair of his own. "I am Kenny's Karamazov father," Kepesh declares, once again demonstrating his penchant for using literature to comprehend his relationships, "the base, the monstrous force with whom he, a saint of love, a man who must behave well all the time, feels himself wronged and parricidal, as though he were all the brothers Karamazov in one" (78). Kepesh attempts to assuage his son's guilt—to encourage him to "find [force]" so that he can enjoy an unconstrained sexual life—but the son, not surprisingly, rejects his father's advice. "My son can fuck only a girl with the right moral credentials," Kepesh jokes. "Please, I tell him, it's a perversity no better or worse than any other. Recognize it for what it is and don't feel so special" (88). Despite his attempts to dismiss his son's moralizing, Kepesh cannot so easily counter Kenny's critique of his behavior, of the way Kepesh uses the social and cultural upheaval of the late 1960s to justify his decision to leave his first marriage. It's an argument that Kenny directly makes in one of the enraged letters he sends his father: "In my mind, I tried to excuse you, I tried to understand you. But the *sixties*? That explosion of childishness, that vulgar, mindless, collective regression, and that explains everything and excuses it all? Can't you come up with any better alibi?" (90).

Beyond Kepesh's pontification, his reading of history that elevates his sexual life as an embodiment of a vital strain of American life, his confessions throughout *The Dying Animal* capture the ways in which sexual desire continues to unravel his sense of himself. Now in his sixties, Kepesh is in no way past sex, and its presence threatens to rupture the masculine identity that he has constructed. "Yet what do you do if you're sixty-two and believe you'll never have a claim on something so perfect again," Kepesh asks early in the narrative. "What do you do if you're sixty-two and the urge to take whatever is still takable couldn't be stronger? What do you do if you're sixty-two and you realize that all those bodily parts invisible up to now (kidneys, lungs, veins, arteries, brain, intestines, prostate, heart) are about to start making themselves distressingly apparent, while the organ most conspicuous throughout your life is doomed to dwindle into insignificance" (33–4). As Shostak notes, Roth in *The Dying Animal* "unmasks the naked narcissism behind such masculine desire, a narcissism that readily accepts the objectification of the women who fulfill that desire."[10] Indeed, *The Dying Animal* remains one of Roth's most disquieting reads, as Kepesh meticulously and gratuitously describes his sexual escapades with Consuela—recalling how he once pinned her down and "fucked her mouth" and "kept her fixed there, kept her steady by holding her hair, by turning a twist of hair in one hand and wrapping it round my fist like a thong, like a strap, like the reins that fasten to the bit of a bridle" and then she bit back at him, a gesture of untamed violence that Kepesh relishes (30). The excessiveness of the graphic detail in Kepesh's narrative—the verbal attention he lavishes on preserving Consuela's body, her "gorgeous breasts" and "sleek pubic hair" (28)—not only confirms his perpetual objectification of women, but also illustrates the ways the realities of sex and death intertwine and threaten to collapse his self-image as a liberated man. "This need. This derangement," he laments after Consuela breaks off their relationship because Kepesh fails to show up at her graduation party. "Will it never stop? I don't even know after a while what I'm desperate for. Her tits? Her soul? Her youth? Her simple mind? Maybe it's worse than that—maybe now that I'm nearing death, I also long secretly not to be free" (106).

Kepesh's crisis culminates in *The Dying Animal*'s final movement when Consuela suddenly reenters Kepesh's life after she has been diagnosed with breast cancer. She asks Kepesh to take photographs of her breasts before she has a double mastectomy, allowing Kepesh one more opportunity to bestow attention on the part of her body that has so preoccupied his thoughts. The scene cleverly brings the Kepesh trilogy full circle, the man who once turned into a breast now memorializing them for a woman who is about to have hers surgically removed. "But the erotic power of Consuela's body—well, that is over," Kepesh acknowledges after photographing her topless. "Yes, that night I'd had an erection, but I couldn't have sustained it. I'm fortunate enough to have a hard-on and the drive, but I would have been in great trouble if she had asked me to sleep with her that night" (142). This confession is, in many ways, Kepesh's most shocking utterance, a seemingly callous remark that suggests how he sees women's bodies as simply vessels for his pleasure. Yet, the scene, with Consuela performing a striptease more for herself than for Kepesh, remains vital to the complicated sexual politics that *The Dying Animal* pursues. As Shostak argues, "While the scene is uncomfortable because of all the meanings it conventionally arouses, however, Roth uses it to contradict those meanings, primarily to protect female pleasure and not to instigate male pleasure."[11]

The trilogy concludes with Consuela calling Kepesh in the middle of the night, asking him to visit her before she has the surgery to remove her breasts. "I have to go," Kepesh tells his nameless conversational partner. "She wants me to sleep in the bed with here there. She has not eaten all day. She has to eat. She has to be fed. You? Stay if you wish. If you want to stay, if you want to leave . . . Look, there is not time, I must run!" (156). Kepesh's panicked exit, however, is interrupted by his guest, who speaks for the first time. "Don't go," the other voice enjoins Kepesh in the novel's closing passage. "Think about it. Think. Because if you go, you're finished" (156). This indefinite conclusion— a reversal of Dr. Spielvogel's famous "punchline" at the end of *Portnoy's Complaint* ("Now vee may perhaps to begin. Yes?")—intimates Kepesh's collapse at the prospect of committing himself to help Consuela through her illness. Kepesh's self-image as an independent man breaks down at the reality of death that Consuela's illness embodies. He is not so much undone by sexual desire, which was at the root of his initial fear of his relationship with Consuela, as he is by the need for human connection, a need that he has steadfastly rejected through his adult life. If *The Breast* began Kepesh's saga with one inexplicable and unexpected transformation, *The Dying Animal* ends the trilogy on a similar, if more disquieting note. Roth purposely refuses to resolve the narrative in this conclusion—we can only guess whether Kepesh stays or follows his instinct to help Consuela—but either way, Kepesh's identity dissolves in this moment. He is not so much transformed as he is undone. That the novel concludes with the anonymous voice and not Kepesh's, whose voice has dominated these three books, is a significant gesture, hinting at how Kepesh finally dissipates as a character, broken by the realities of death and the inevitable failings of the human body.

CHAPTER 5

Personality Crisis
The "Roth" Tetralogy

In the opening of *The Facts: A Writer's Autobiography* (1988), Roth comments on "a breakdown" that impelled him to write the memoir. "Although there's no need to delve into particulars here," Roth confesses, "I will tell you that in the spring of 1987, at the height of a ten-year period of creativity, what was to have been minor surgery turned into a prolonged physical ordeal that led to an extreme depression that carried me right to the edge of emotional and mental dissolution" (5). The crisis was triggered by the sleeping pill Halcion, which Roth had been prescribed after suffering a knee injury while swimming in 1987. The medicine, as Claudia Roth Pierpont reports, "brought on a panoply of horrific side effects [in Roth]: hallucinations, panic attacks, and ultimately a suicidal depression that went on for four months before the symptoms were traced to their source."[1] In addition to the Halcion-induced breakdown, Roth underwent quintuple bypass surgery in 1989; later that year his father, Herman, succumbed at age eighty-eight to a brain tumor.[2] "Life suddenly interrupted literature," Ira Nadel writes of Roth's experience during the late 1980s, "and, try as he might, 'thinking in straight lines'—a phrase used by the critic Alfred Kazin—was impossible."[3]

The four books that Roth produced during this tumultuous period—*The Facts: A Writer's Autobiography*, *Deception: A Novel* (1990), *Patrimony: A True Story* (1991), and *Operation Shylock: A Confession* (1993)—remain the most idiosyncratic and challenging works of his career. Throughout this sequence, Roth abandons the alter-egos that have dominated his fiction since *My Life as a Man*, choosing instead to make himself the central character of his work. By considering these books as a discrete series, which I will refer to as the Roth tetralogy, this chapter will consider how the tetralogy marks Roth's most complex engagement with the connection between his own identity and the act of writing, one that deepens the exploration of identity pursued in *The Counterlife*.[4] Roth's decision to subtitle each book in the series, purposely identifying its mode, reflects how these works play off one another like different movements within a musical sequence, each book complicating the notion of identity that the previous entry embraced.[5] In juxtaposing the "facts" with "deception," the straightforwardness of *Patrimony* with the mischief of *Operation Shylock*, Roth constructs a conception of selfhood that is more complex than the postmodern denial of self that Zuckerman posits at the conclusion of *The Counterlife*. While the tetralogy does not resolve the tension between fact and fiction, it ultimately creates a structure that holds the contradictory positions that Roth wants to explore, without endorsing one over the others.

That Roth would begin this sequence with a book that tried to establish "the facts" of his life is not surprising. The book's five chapters dutifully record the major circumstances that shaped Roth's life through the age of thirty-five: his childhood in Newark; his experience attending Bucknell University; his problematic first marriage to Margaret Martinson Williams (whom Roth refers to as "Josie" in the book); the charges of being a self-hating Jew that *Goodbye, Columbus* generated; and the creative and commercial breakthrough of *Portnoy's Complaint*. While there are a few interesting revelations, notably Roth's recollection of the anti-Semitic protests that infiltrated his otherwise idyllic Newark childhood, *The Facts* largely eschews the confessional impulse that informs most autobiographies. Even when Roth recounts the horrors of his first marriage, in the section sardonically entitled "Girl of My Dreams," *The Facts* remains largely placid, especially when contrasted with Roth's fierce treatment of the marriage in *My Life as a Man*. "Undermining experience, embellishing experience, rearranging and enlarging experience into a species of mythology —after thirty years at that, it could have seemed like I'd had enough even under the best of circumstances," Roth writes in the letter to Zuckerman that opens the book. "To demythologize myself and play it straight, to pair the facts as lived with facts as presented might well have seemed the next thing to do—if not the only thing I *could* do—so long as the capacity for self-transformation and, with it, the imagination were at the point of collapse" (7).

That said, *The Facts* does not present an objective view of Roth's early years or the forces that shaped him as a writer. "You search your past with certain questions on your mind," Roth confesses early in the memoir, "indeed, you search out your past to discover which events have led you to asking those specific questions. It isn't that you subordinate your ideas to the force of the facts in autobiography but that you construct a sequence of stories to bind up the facts with a persuasive *hypothesis* that unravels your history's meaning" (8). Throughout the book, Roth presents himself as a high-minded, if somewhat naïve, young man who is frequently the victim of others' unreasonable behavior: his father's irrational fear that some harm will come to his youngest son when he starts college (an anxiety that Roth repurposed in *Indignation*); the rigid sexual mores that inhibited his sexual life as an undergraduate at Bucknell; the narrowmindedness of the Jewish readers who misread his fiction; the hyperbolic lies that his first wife concocted—most notably, feigning a pregnancy and an abortion so that Roth would marry her (an episode that he would use in *My Life as a Man*).

Roth, however, brilliantly complicates this rather staid self-image in the book's final section, where Nathan Zuckerman responds to the manuscript and urges Roth not to publish it. "Where's the anger," Zuckerman correctly points out. "You suggest that the anger developed *after* Josie, a result of her insanely destructive possessiveness and then the punishment handed out by the court. . . . I could be wrong, but you've got to prove it, to convince me that early on you didn't find something insipid about the Jewish experience as you knew it, insipid about the middle class as you experienced it, insipid about marriage and domesticity, insipid even about love" (171). Zuckerman's rebuttal reveals all that is unconvincing about Roth's self-presentation in *The Facts*, his critique underscoring that the facts, stripped of imagination, reveal very little. "Your acquaintance with the facts, your sense of the facts, is much less developed than your understanding, your intuitive weighing and balancing of fiction," Zuckerman argues at the beginning of his section. "You make a fictional world that is far more exciting than the world it comes out of. My guess is that you've written metamorphoses of yourself so many times, you no longer have any idea what *you* are or ever were. By now what you are is a walking text" (162). While Zuckerman's advice not to publish is self-interested (he is, after all, arguing for the necessity of his existence), he posits a compelling argument that locates the vitality that is largely absent from the text. Zuckerman's letter also enables Roth to control the book's reception, masking what is essential an apologia for his personal life (particularly his relationship with his first wife) and his work as simply an assemblage of "the facts." To read Zuckerman's letter as the final word on the subject would be to ignore what Roth accomplishes through the juxtaposition of fact and fiction that the book as whole offers—a juxtaposition that anticipates the experiments Roth will perform over the course over the rest of the tetralogy.

The following two "Roth" books, *Deception* and *Patrimony*, mark the opposing extremes of the series, deepening the tension between autobiography and fiction that *The Facts* illuminated. On the surface, *Deception* returns to familiar Roth territory as it records the pre- and post-coital conversations of a middle-aged writer, named Philip, with an unnamed Englishwoman who resembles the Maria character in *The Counterlife*. (The novel contains Philip's conversations with other women, most notably a Czechoslovakian woman, but the bulk of the novel is focused on the affair with the Englishwoman.) Despite its overly familiar subject matter, *Deception* continues the formal experimentation that had characterized *The Ghost Writer* and *The Counterlife*. *Deception* consists only of dialogue; there is no exposition or narration, and the novel reads like a play stripped of its stage directions.

While Roth's fiction has always been interested in voice—his ability to capture his characters' love of talking is one of his great strengths as a novelist—the dialogue in *Deception* remains more succinct and playful. The page-long rants that frequently occur in Roth's fiction are replaced by the more measured and contained language that the adulterous couple shares. In one of the more amusing and revealing episodes, Philip's lover playfully recounts all the charges of misogyny that have been leveled against Roth in his career. "People like you are not treated kindly if found guilty, and for good reason," Philip's lover asserts. "You are one with the mass of men who caused women great suffering and extreme humiliation—humiliation from which they are only now being delivered, thanks to the untiring work of courts such as this one. Why did you publish books that cause women suffering? Didn't you think that those writings could be used against us by our enemies?" (114). The scene is amusing as Roth confronts the misogyny charges in a seduction scene—the scene ends with the couple making love—in a way that attempts to strip those charges of their seriousness and weight (117). The move is also typical of how hard *Deception* works to convince its readers that it's somehow providing a glimpse of the "real" Roth, that what we are reading is not fiction, but instead Roth's uncensored notes.

Indeed, Roth's decision to implicate himself as the novel's adulterous protagonist—at the time, Roth was in a relationship with the actress Claire Bloom (whom he would marry soon after its publication)—remains central to the argument he pursues in the novel. "I portray myself as implicated because it is not enough just to be present," Philip declares late in the novel. "That's not the way I go about it. To compromise some 'character' doesn't get me where I want to be. What heats things up is compromising me. It kind of makes the indictment juicer, besmirching myself" (183–4). Despite being pitched as his "most original work of fiction about the erotic life since *Portnoy's Complaint*," *Deception* is not a rewrite of Roth's earlier fiction. The novel has little interest in sex or adultery, but instead focuses on the duplicity that is an inherent part of storytelling. Throughout the Zuckerman Bound series, Roth continually flirted with the line separating fact and fiction, but *Deception* heightens the games he played with readers in his earlier Zuckerman novels. Midway through *Deception*, Philip comments on a proposed sequel to *The Counterlife*, imagining a plot where a young biographer struggles to construct Zuckerman's life story after Nathan's death, a narrative thread that the real Roth would later repurpose in *Exit Ghost*. "What interests [the imagined biographer] is the terrible ambiguity of the 'I,' the way a writer makes a myth of himself and, particularly, *why*," Philip muses to his lover. "What started it? Where do they come from, all these improvisations on a self?" (98). These questions percolate throughout *Deception* as Roth plays with the line between fact and fiction; the novel is ultimately a bewildering hall-of-mirrors that pretends to be the sort of unvarnished notes that Roth presented in *The Facts*. "I write fiction and I'm told it's autobiography," Philip declares late in the novel. "I write autobiography and I'm told it's fiction, so since I'm so dim and they're so smart, let *them* decide what it is or it isn't" (190).

In its penultimate section, Philip's longtime romantic partner discovers the notebook recording his conversations with his lover; in the ensuing fight, Philip argues for the preservation of the conventional divide between autobiographical truth and imaginative creation—Philip emphatically tells his partner that the woman in the notebook is only "*words*—and try as I will, I cannot fuck words!" (192). The fight returns to the ethics of writing fiction that Roth explored in *The Ghost Writer* and *The Counterlife*, as Philip's partner asserts that the book's publication would "humiliate" her even if the woman depicted in the notebooks is completely imagined. "But discretion is, unfortunately, not for novelists," Philip retorts. "Neither is shame. *Feeling* shame is automatic in me, inescapable, it may even be *good*; it's a yielding to shame that's the serious crime" (190–1). It's a credo that Roth has asserted since *Portnoy's Complaint*, and *Deception* asserts the novelist's duty to be as "shameless" as possible. The novel's final section, however, unsettles this reading as Philip's final conversation with the Englishwoman reveals her to be the model for Maria in *The Counterlife*, a move that demolishes the distinction he made in the previous section. Is *Deception* autobiography or fiction? The book ultimately provides no solution, the title referring not to the betrayal that adultery occasions, but instead to Roth's deception, proffering the possibility of truth, only to deny the reader any access to a definitive reading of the text.

The metafictional confusion produced by *Deception* might suggest that Roth has resolved the tension between autobiographical truth and imaginary construct by demolishing the line separating the two, aligning himself firmly on the side of postmodern indeterminacy. While *Deception* reveals storytelling to be a problematic, if not a dubious act, Roth's next book, *Patrimony*, reaffirms its value—the book's subtitle, "A True Story," suggesting narrative's ability to both recapture the past and convey life's most difficult truths. As a testament to the father who was both a natural storyteller and unrelenting on himself and everyone he encountered, *Patrimony* forgoes the narrative experiments that defined Roth's previous novels and stands as his most unflinching and affecting book. Contrasting *Patrimony* with Roth's fiction since *The Counterlife*, Mark Shechner amusingly remarks, "The 'self' may be something you put together afresh everyday, or every book, especially if you are writer for whom self-consciousness is the breakfast cereal of your profession. But your father is *your father*, and postmodernism and magic realism simply won't do."[6] Unlike *The Facts*, *Patrimony* fully depicts the pain and messiness of existence. In the memoir's most memorable passage, Roth must clean up his father's excrement after Herman has had an explosive bowel movement. "So *that* was the patrimony," Roth writes. "And not because cleaning it up was symbolic of something else but because it wasn't, because it was nothing less or more than the lived reality that it was." (176). By emphasizing the "shit," the impact of the "facts" of existence makes itself fully felt. *Patrimony* does not nullify the postmodern experiments of the previous two books, but instead it insists, with the doggedness of Herman Roth, on the presence and efficacy of "lived reality" and on writing's ability to render that "reality" accurately.

The finale to the tetralogy, *Operation Shylock*, does not resolve the tension between fact and fiction explored throughout the series, but instead stands as the series' comic culmination, an overstuffed work that pushes Roth's engagement with his own identity, as well as the limits of realistic fiction, to their breaking point. One of the novel's epigraphs comes from Genesis 32, where Jacob wrestles the unidentified man, an allusion that suggests the crisis of self that Roth has been struggling with over the course of the tetralogy lacks any definite resolution or explanation. More so than even *Deception*, where Roth gave the protagonist his first name and history, *Operation Shylock* deliberately blurs the line between fact and fiction: the book begins with a character by the name of Philip Roth recounting his recent Halcion-induced breakdown. The novel centers on Philip's discovery of an imposter Philip Roth, a man who physically resembles Philip and who has been going around Israel advocating for Diasporism, a movement that advocates for Jews to leave Israel and return to Europe. Despite the outlandish nature of the doppelgänger's plot, Philip finds the imposter's intrusion to be reinvigorating. By identifying his imposter as his Moishe Pipik, a figure from Jewish folklore whose name translates as Moses Bellybutton, Philip renders him a ridiculous but necessary component of existence—like a bellybutton, the imposter becomes a rather absurd marker of one's existence and identity.

As the premise suggests, *Operation Shylock* extends the postmodern tricks of *The Counterlife* and *Deception*; the novel's preface contends that the book, subtitled *A Confession*, comes from Roth's notebook and "is as accurate an account as I am able to give of actual occurrences that I lived through during my middle fifties and that culminated, early in 1988, in my agreeing to undertake an intelligence-gathering operation for Israel's foreign intelligence service, the Mossad" (13). Roth is clearly having a great deal of fun in *Operation Shylock*, imagining himself in the novel's conclusion to be a Mossad operative engaged in a clandestine operation meant to further Israeli interests. While the book is tremendously entertaining, one of his final books to be legitimately funny, it also remains Roth's most crowded and antic novel. As John Updike quipped in his review, the characters all "seem to be on speed," and the novel contains Roth's most dense dialogue.[7] Unlike the sharp exchanges in *Deception*, the characters in *Operation Shylock* can't stop talking. The novel also contains prolonged excepts from Roth's actual interview with the Israeli author Aharon Appelfeld, which were first published in the *New York Times Book Review* and later collected in *Shop Talk* (2001), as well as Roth's notes from the 1988 trial of John Demjanjuk, the Ukrainian American who was accused of being "Ivan the Terrible," the notorious watchman who ran the gas chamber at the Treblinka extermination camp. The variety of the sources—some real, some imagined—extend the narrative questions that Roth asked in *Deception* about the line separating fact from fiction, but here the stakes are significantly raised as Roth considers the legacy of the Holocaust and the meaning of the state of Israel.

Despite its exhaustive quality, *Operation Shylock* nevertheless remains a vital work in Roth's oeuvre, deepening the notion of identity that Roth wrestled with throughout the tetralogy as well as engaging with the larger historical question that would propel the American Trilogy. The Demjanjuk trial—in 1988, Demjanjuk was convicted of being "Ivan the Terrible," but his conviction would later be overturned, though in 2011 he was convicted in Germany of having been a guard at the Sobibor extermination camp[8]—is the more serious counternarrative to Philip's comic encounters with his Pipik. In Demjanjuk, Roth finds a terrifying example of how impossible it is to know another person—is Demjanjuk an innocent retired factory worker, or a horrific mass murderer, or both? "So there he was. Or wasn't," Philip thinks as he watches Demjanjuk at the trial, suggesting how inscrutable other people ultimately remain (62). The contested nature of Demjanjuk's identity illustrates what Nathan Zuckerman will later assert in *American Pastoral*: "The fact remains that getting people right is not what living is all about anyway. It's getting them wrong that is living, getting them wrong and wrong and wrong and then, on careful reconsideration, getting them wrong again. That's how we know we're alive: we're wrong" (35).

Roth's depiction of the trial in *Operation Shylock* signals the novel's broader interest in the question of Israel, a question that he has previously taken up in the "Judea" section of *The Counterlife*. In that novel, Nathan Zuckerman's brother, Henry, abandons his life as a dentist back in New Jersey and reinvents his life in a West Bank settlement. Roth's treatment of Israel in *Operation Shylock* is much more expansive, and the novel, alongside *I Married a Communist*, remains Roth's most overtly political work as it attempts to capture a multitude of opinions on Israel's place in the world. The views expressed in *Operation Shylock* range from the outrage of George Ziad, a former friend of Philip's from his student days at the University of Chicago, who has returned home to the West Bank, to the more knowing pragmatism of Smilesburger, the older Mossad agent who holds no illusions that he could be convicted as a war criminal if the Palestinians were ever to come into power. A young Israeli lieutenant who was detained for visiting Ziad tells Philip, just after reading *The Ghost Writer,* "I know what reality is. I'm not a fool who believes that he is pure or that life is simple. It is Israel's fate to live in an Arab sea. Jews accepted this fate rather than having nothing and no fate. Jews accepted partition and the Arabs did not. If they'd said yes, my father [an Auschwitz survivor] reminds me, they would be celebrating forty years of statehood too. But every political decision with which they have been confronted, invariably they have made the wrong choice. *I know all this.* Nine tenths of their misery they owe to the idiocy of their own political leaders. *I know that.* But still I look at my own government and want to vomit" (169–70).

While Philip comes through *Operation Shylock* rejuvenated, the prospects for both Israelis and Palestinians look far less assured. Philip muses to Smilesburger at the end of the novel, "Nothing is secure. Man the pillar of instability" (393), a lesson that will reverberate throughout much of Roth's later fiction as he begins to consider how history can unexpectedly transform a life. Although the political outlook remains bleak, *Operation Shylock* brings the Roth tetralogy to a comedic conclusion, the novel ending with a restored Philip able to move forward after his encounter with his Pipik, who mysteriously disappears, and his brief sojourn as a Mossad agent. "It's a happy book, as I read it," Philip's Mossad handler Smilesburger reminds him in the novel's final pages. "Happiness radiates from it. There are all kinds of ordeals and trials but it's about someone who is recovering. . . . It's a comedy in the classic sense. He [Philip] comes through it *all* unscathed" (394). Roth by the end of the tetralogy would appear similarly invigorated, his imagination liberated. In the novels that would immediately follow the tetralogy, *Sabbath's Theater* and *American*

Pastoral, Roth would move away from the postmodern hi-jinks that have characterized *Deception* and *Operation Shylock* and return to the sort of realism, although one infused by the postmodern notion that all narrative is unreliable, that he practiced at the very start of his career. Freed from the confines of the self, Roth began to look outward (and backward) in his fiction, grappling with the history that has shaped his life as an American.

CHAPTER 6

Back in the USA

Sabbath's Theater and the American Trilogy

As the "American century" came to a close, Philip Roth enjoyed a creative renewal that resulted in his emergence, alongside Toni Morrison and John Updike, as one of his generation's most decorated novelists. Starting with *Sabbath's Theater* (1995) and continuing through the American Trilogy (*American Pastoral* [1997], *I Married a Communist* [1998], and *The Human Stain* [2000]), Roth's fiction expanded to survey the historical events and forces that had transformed the United States during his lifetime. "When I came home from England for good in '89, it was really my rediscovering America as a writer," he explained in a 2000 interview with Charles McGrath. "I came back, in fact, because I felt out of touch. Not that I didn't know what was going on here from reading the paper, but what was missing was the daily immediacy of what people were saying and thinking—missing was everything that was going on by the way."[1] With the exception of the brief *The Dying Animal* (2001), the novels that Roth produced in the decade following *Operation Shylock* were the most robust and critically well-received of his career.[2] *Sabbath's Theater* secured Roth his second National Book Award (his first had come thirty-five years earlier for *Goodbye, Columbus*), *American Pastoral* was awarded the Pulitzer Prize, and *The Human Stain* won the PEN/Faulkner Award.[3]

On the ambitiousness of the American Trilogy, Greil Marcus argues that "Roth took up a patriotic literary project that in the United States had no contemporary match in any field: not in the movies, not in music, certainly not in the work of any other novelist, young or, like Roth, old—old but, in his mid- and late sixties, doing his most ambitious work."[4] Marcus's assessment is only one instance of the enthusiastic critical reception that this sequence received.

When in 2006 the *New York Times* published a list of the best American novels of the past twenty-five years, *American Pastoral* came in second, falling only behind Toni Morrison's *Beloved* (1987), a sign of how firmly Roth's later work had been canonized within a relatively short amount of time. In his introductory essay to the list, A.O. Scott commented on this critical tendency to privilege Roth's later work, acknowledging that "the Roth whose primary concern is the past—the elegiac, summarizing, conservative Roth—is preferred over his more aesthetically radical, restless, present-minded doppelgänger by a narrow but decisive margin."[5] Yet, as David Gooblar has argued, "the 'American trilogy' shows many continuities with the rest of Roth's work, exhibiting preoccupations that have drawn Roth's scrutiny for more than 40 years."[6] Gooblar's reading here is compelling; the American Trilogy and *Sabbath's Theater* do not mark a departure for Roth—as Gooblar points out, these novels revisit questions of "self-determination and social determination" that were at the heart of *Goodbye, Columbus*[7]—but instead signal a deepening of Roth's fictive approach. To this point, Debra Shostak maintains that "these novels explore in new ways all of the main concerns to which Roth devotes his previous fiction, but they do so within the context of his intimacy with the events and people of the later twentieth century in the United States, and also with an intense sense of place, most often the Newark, New Jersey of Roth's youth."[8]

That this triumphant period of Roth's career should begin with *Sabbath's Theater*—his most scandalous book since *Portnoy's Complaint*—is worth emphasizing. The novel stands as his most sexually explicit, but it's also one of his most accomplished, a forceful return to realism after the more postmodern experiments of *The Counterlife* and *Operation Shylock*. As a protagonist, the libidinous Mickey Sabbath, a sixty-four-year-old disgraced puppeteer who revels in transgression, liberated Roth's imagination. The novel pivots between Sabbath's misadventures in 1994 as he returns, after a three-decade absence, to New York City and his memories of his past, memories that nearly overwhelm Sabbath as the novel progresses. Envisioning his obituary, Sabbath imagines his final days as an "extravaganza" entitled "*Farewell to a Half Century of Masturbation*" (193) ending with the punchline, "Mr. Sabbath did nothing for Israel" (195). After leaving his second wife, who harbors fantasies of castrating him, Sabbath contemplates suicide as he mourns the death of his longtime mistress, Drenka Balich, an innkeeper who immigrated from Croatia and whose taste for sexual adventure matched Sabbath's erotic appetite. Beyond Drenka's death from cancer, Sabbath is haunted by the memories of his mother; his older brother, Morty, who was shot down over the Philippines during the Second World War; and his first wife, Nikki, who mysteriously disappeared in 1964. Compounding these losses, Sabbath is also hobbled by arthritis and unemployed since losing his job as a college instructor after getting involved with a student who records one of their lurid phone sex sessions.

For all its obsession with death, *Sabbath's Theater* stands as one of Roth's most comic and exhilarating performances, and Sabbath ultimately refuses to succumb to his suicidal impulses. "The news was for people to talk about, and Sabbath, indifferent to the untransgressive run of normalized pursuits, did not wish to talk to people," Roth writes of Sabbath's single-minded pursuit of transgression. "He didn't care who was at war with whom or where a plane had crashed or what had befallen Bangladesh. He didn't even want to know who the president was of the United States. He'd rather fuck Drenka, he'd rather fuck *anyone*, than watch Tom Brokaw. His range of pleasure was narrow and never did extend to the evening news. Sabbath was reduced the way a sauce is reduced, boiled down by his burners, the better to concentrate his essence and be defiantly himself" (126). Much like Nathan Zuckerman, who at the end of *The Counterlife* declares that he is nothing more than a series of impersonations, Sabbath embraces the performative nature of identity. Indeed, Sabbath remains the most performative of all of Roth's male protagonists: his performance is a reaction to all his losses, and it masks the question of what real identity exists beneath the traumas that shape our sense of the world and ourselves. "The law of living: fluctuation," Sabbath thinks as he steals the panties of his former theater associate's nineteen-year-old daughter so that he can masturbate to them. "For every thought a counterthought, for every urge a counterurge. No wonder you either go crazy and die or decide to disappear" (158).

Despite its profanity, the novel remains a deeply felt meditation on longing and loss, capturing the ways in which the dead continually haunt us. Indeed, the past overwhelms the present moment in *Sabbath's Theater* as Sabbath obsesses over the losses that have defined his life. In a moving scene late in the novel, Sabbath visits the cemetery where his family is buried. The sequence, which Roth highlighted in "The Ruthless Intimacy of Fiction" (2013) as one of his favorites, remains one of the most emotionally charged moments in his fiction, as Sabbath recalls his grandmother, whose memory becomes a conduit to recapture the experience of growing up with his older brother Morty on the Jersey Shore:

> Whenever we went out fishing, you couldn't wait for us to get back so you could clean the catch. Used to catch shiners. Weighed less than a pound. You'd fry four or five of them in a pan. Very bony but great. Watching you eat a shiner was a lot of fun, too, for everyone but Mother. What else did we bring you to clean? Fluke, flounder, when we fished Shark River inlet. Weakfish. That's about it. When Morty joined the Air Corps, the night before he left we went down to the beach with our rods for an hour. Never

got into the gear as kids. Just fished. Rod, hooks, sinkers, line, sometimes lures, mostly bait, mostly squid. That was it. Heavy-duty tackle. Big barbed hook. Never cleaned the rod. Once a summer splashed some water on it. Keep the same rig on the whole time. Just change the sinkers and the bait if we wanted to fish on the bottom. We went down to the beach to fish for an hour. Everybody in the house was crying because he was going to war the next day. You were already here. You were gone. (367)

Sabbath's language throughout the passage is spare; the emphasis is on getting the exact details right, not on embellishing them. Embedded in this sequence is Roth's argument for what realistic fiction can do: the way in which the right detail can capture all that is ephemeral and wonderful about our existence. That said, Sabbath's memories cannot resurrect the dead; the novel insists on the utter reality of death, the way in which it eventually nullifies all our memories. While language cannot resurrect the dead, it is our only mechanism through which we can process our grief; it gives shape to all the losses we encounter in a lifetime. "We are immoderate because grief is immoderate," Roth writes later in the novel, "all the hundreds and thousands of kinds of grief" (407).

Beyond its fascination with grief, *Sabbath's Theater* insists on history's ability to shape one's existence. For Sabbath, history comes in the form of Morty's death in the Second World War, a loss that destroys his mother and profoundly changes Sabbath's sense of the world. "Through the blow of death Sabbath is edified way ahead of his time by the crises that are born of contingency," Roth notes in "The Ruthless Intimacy of Fiction." "He is transformed utterly at the age of fifteen by the unimaginable made gruesomely real, when everything essential to life disappears in a blink" (*Why Write?* 397). Visiting Morty's grave, Sabbath contemplates the way our actual existence always confounds our sense of what *should* happen: "King of the kingdom of the unillusioned, emperor of no expectations, crestfallen man-god of the double cross, Sabbath had *still* to learn that nothing but *nothing* will ever turn out—and this obtuseness was, in itself, a deep, deep shock" (359). It is a lesson that Roth will explore throughout the American Trilogy, as he considers how the inexplicable whims of history can annihilate an existence. Toward the novel's conclusion, Sabbath wraps himself up in the American flag that his family was given when Morty was killed: "He took the flag down with him onto the beach. There he unfurled it, a flag with forty-eight stars, wrapped himself up in it, and, in the mist there, wept and wept" (407). The image of the mourning Sabbath, draped in the American flag of his childhood, perfectly captures the sense of loss, an immense trauma triggered by historical happenstance, that propels *Sabbath's Theater* and the subsequent American Trilogy. Nevertheless, *Sabbath's Theater* does not succumb to easy nostalgia, nor does it reject the present moment, as Sabbath remains unable to kill himself. "And [Sabbath] couldn't do it. He could not fucking die," Roth writes in the novel's concluding lines after Sabbath has been caught urinating on Drenka's grave by her outraged son, Matthew, a state trooper. "How could he leave? How could he go? Everything he hated was here" (451). That Sabbath continues on, that his compulsive need to transgress cannot be killed, is central to Roth's argument in the novel: the reality of death cannot strip existence of its exuberance. The impulses Sabbath embodies—to antagonize, to perform, to play—will persist.

Following *Sabbath's Theater*'s critical success, Roth quickly embarked on his next project, the American Trilogy, a sequence that would win him substantial critical praise and secure his place in American letters. Published at the end of the century, the sequence does not attempt to present a more definitive account of the United States' postwar history, but instead considers the narratives, the myths and countermyths, that have shaped the nation's sense of itself. In its foregrounding of history, the trilogy remains acutely aware of our inability to ever fully know another person or to come to an unmediated understanding of the past. In reconsidering how the history of the postwar nation has been narrated, Roth turned to his most-employed alter-ego, Nathan Zuckerman. Zuckerman, who was last seen in *The Facts* arguing with his creator over whether Roth should publish his memoir, remains at the heart of the American Trilogy: it is through his history and sensibility that Roth considers the United States' recent past.

Whereas in the earlier Zuckerman novels Roth employed the character as a way of reimagining the circumstances that had shaped his own career as a novelist, in these later novels Roth uses him to imagine both other characters' lives—Seymour "The Swede" Levov in *American Pastoral*, Ira Ringold in *I Married a Communist*, and Coleman Silk in *The Human Stain*—and the period of history through which he has lived. Roth's selection of these historical crises—the McCarthy era, the unrest over the Vietnam War, and the Clinton/Lewinsky scandal—makes sense, as each moment helps illuminate the contradictory forces that have run throughout American history. "What we know is that, in an unclichéd way, nobody knows anything," Zuckerman muses in *The Human Stain*. "You *can't* know anything. The things you *know* you don't know. Intention? Motive? Consequence? Meaning? All that we don't know is astonishing. Even more astonishing is what passes for knowing" (209). In a similar moment in *American Pastoral* that could serve as the thesis statement for the entire trilogy, Zuckerman asserts, "The fact remains that getting people right is not what living is all about anyway. It's getting them wrong that is living, getting them wrong and wrong and wrong and then, on careful reconsideration, getting them wrong again. That's how we know we're alive: we're wrong" (35).

By emphasizing the limitations of narrative and acknowledging the limitations of an individual's imagination, the American Trilogy engages in what Linda Hutcheon has defined as historiographic metafiction. Hutcheon explains: "In most of the critical work on postmodernism, it is narrative—be it in literature, history, or theory—that has usually been the major focus of attention. Historiographic metafiction incorporates all three of these domains: that is, its theoretical self-awareness of history and fiction as human constructs (historio-graphic metafiction) is made the grounds for its rethinking and reworking of the forms and contents of the past."[9] The American Trilogy, as historiographic metafiction, questions the stories that we choose to tell to account for our past, and it exposes how history—that is, a narrative understanding of the past—is constructed. Narrative, for Roth, cannot fully resolve the past—cannot simplify it or explain it away—but it offers us a singular means through which we can speculate, play with the different possibilities of why things happened the way they did. For in the end, these three novels do not explain America's postwar history—there is no clear lesson or moral to the series—but they instead illuminate the problematic role that narrative has in shaping our sense of history and our sense of ourselves. What Roth would seem to be asking in these novels is: how do we make sense of our national history once the veil of innocence has been lifted? How do we move forward once we have become estranged from our sense of ourselves and our nation? These are the unanswerable questions that Roth pursues throughout the American Trilogy.

That Roth should begin his evaluation of postwar America by revisiting the unrest of the 1960s makes a certain amount of sense, as the social and political upheaval of those years—in particular, the protests over the war in Vietnam—were the pivotal crises that reoriented his sense of his nation. As early as 1974, Roth described the 1960s as "the demythologizing decade" where "much that had been considered in my own brief lifetime to be disgraceful and disgusting forced itself upon the national consciousness, loathsome or not; what was assumed to be beyond reproach became the target of blasphemous assault; what was imagined to be indestructible, impermeable, in the very nature of American things, yielded and collapsed overnight" (Reading Myself 87–8). The sense of "sudden collapse" that Roth describes here is worth highlighting, suggesting the ways in which the protests of those years, as well as the violent rhetoric of more radical groups like the Weather Underground and the Black Panthers, inspired Roth to reconsider his beliefs about the United States' self-professed moral superiority.

While *Portnoy's Complaint* has been frequently cited as spurring on the cultural tumult of those years, Roth's response to the events of the late 1960s was more complicated. In a 1974 self-interview, he advanced a more nuanced argument, contending that his generation was uniquely positioned to experience the upheaval of those years: "To have been trained to be a patriotic schoolchild on the rhetoric of World War II, to have developed an attachment to this country in good part on the basis of the myth (*and* reality) of that wartime America made my own spiritual entanglement with *this* wartime America probably more like Lyndon Johnson's than Jerry Rubin's. That I came eventually to despise Johnson did not mean that I was impervious, ever, to his sense, which I took to be genuine, that the America whose leader he was simply could not be on the wrong side, even if for some reason everything seemed to look that way" (*Reading Myself* 89). The ambivalence that Roth describes in that interview can also be felt in his decision to abandon a 1972 manuscript entitled "How the Other Half Lives," which contains the basic plot elements that Roth would return to two decades later when composing *American Pastoral*. In his memoir of his friendship with Roth, Benjamin Taylor reveals that the "germ" for the character who would eventually become Merry Levov in *American Pastoral* was Kathy Boudin, the Weather Underground member convicted of murder in 1980 and "with whose parents, Leonard and Jean Boudin, Roth had been friendly."[10] Patrick Hayes notes, "What is most striking is that the entire story of *American Pastoral*, and all of its characters, were already in place in 1972—but without the idea that the Levov character could be made into the mythic 'Swede,' and without any indication that the story could be narrated as a visionary experience of history, rather than a first-person narrative."[11] In recounting why Roth shelved the original manuscript, Pierpont reveals that the "heroine of Roth's original [1972] story was a New Jersey high school student who blows up the Princeton Library. She was not an entirely unsympathetic character. Back in 1970, Roth tells me, he was so frustrated with the war that— however figuratively—'I was pretty ready to set off a bomb myself.' He had written fifty or sixty pages and got as far as the explosion, but he didn't know where to go from there."[12]

Roth's admission hints at why he might have shelved the manuscript in 1972: he was too emotionally invested in the turmoil of the Vietnam War, and some historical distance was needed to be able to transform the events of that period into fiction. When he returned to the manuscript of "How the Other Half Lives" in the mid-1990s, Roth jettisoned the first-person perspective that he had originally used—Jack Knowles reports the original draft depicts Levov as a sort of "inverted Willy Loman" character[13]—and returned to Nathan

Zuckerman to narrate the Swede's life. The decision to employ Zuckerman as the novel's narrator remains vital to *American Pastoral*'s success, transforming it from a simple historical recreation of one man's experience with the violence that history periodically unleashes and elevating it into a rumination on the contradictory forces that fuel any narrative attempt to understand the past. Over the course of the novel, Zuckerman transforms the guileless and orderly Swede into a contemporary Job, a figure through which Roth reconsiders the legacy of the late 1960s as well as the myths of assimilation and progress that remain fundamental to United States' self-image. "I lifted onto my stage the boy we were all going to follow into America," Zuckerman writes of his reasons for reimagining Levov's life, "our point man into the next immersion, at home here the way the Wasps were at home here, an American not by sheer striving, not by being a Jew who invents a famous vaccine or a Jew on the Supreme Court, not by being the most brilliant or the most eminent or the best" (89).

If the Swede charts out a new path for assimilation into American culture, he also represents a more disciplined notion of masculinity, eschewing the sexual chaos that drives so many of Roth's male protagonists. Indeed, the Swede appears to be the exact opposite of Roth's previous protagonist, the libidinous and profane Mickey Sabbath. As Roth comments in the McGrath interview, Levov is an "orderly man, moderate, kindly, decent by every conventional standard, everything that Sabbath isn't."[14] For the first half of his life, the Swede enjoys a charmed existence that would seem to be a reward for his good-natured constitution, imagining himself as a sort of Johnny Appleseed making his way into the good life that America has to offer. After high school, he has a distinguished stint in the Marines, marries his sweetheart, Dawn, a former Miss New Jersey, and then takes over his father's glove factory, his business success enabling him to vault his family from the urban confines of Newark into the bucolic suburbs of rural New Jersey. After a high school gym coach christened him "the Swede" due to his "brilliant blue gaze and [his] easy, effortless style," the Swede "carried" his nickname "like an invisible passport, all the while wandering deeper into an American's life, forthrightly evolving into a large, smooth, optimistic American such as his conspicuously raw forbears—including the obstinate father whose American claim was not inconsiderable—couldn't have dreamed of as one of their own" (207–8).

The Swede's good fortune and his love affair with America fall apart when his teenaged daughter, Merry, bombs the post office in the local general store to protest the Vietnam War, killing an innocent physician. Merry's violence forces the Swede to acknowledge what his brother, Jerry, so eloquently describes as "the real American crazy shit" (277). "The Swede as he had always known himself—well-meaning, well-behaved, well-ordered Seymour Levov—evaporated, leaving only self-examination in his place," Zuckerman writes of the effect of Merry's crime on the Swede's sense of reality. "He couldn't disentangle himself from the idea that he was responsible any more than he could resort to the devilishly tempting idea that everything was accidental. He had been admitting into a mystery more bewildering even than Merry's stuttering: there was no fluency anywhere. It was *all* stuttering" (93). On the one hand, the bombing shatters the Swede's stable self-image: before the attack, he had perceived things (himself included) as being straightforward and uncomplicated, a complacency that Merry's crime splinters. "Was everyone's brain as unreliable as his," the Swede asks later in the novel. "Was he the only one unable to see what people were up to? Did everyone slip around the way he did, in and out, in and out, a hundred different times a day go from being smart to being smart enough, to being as dumb as the next guy, to being the dumbest bastard who ever lived?" (356). What gives the Swede's epistemological crisis its resonance, however, is the way it coincides with a moment of national uncertainty, when the United States' trajectory suddenly seemed illegible to many Americans. The Swede's uncertainty would seem to be a national condition in the late 1960s and early 1970s, as many Americans struggled to process the traumatic events—the assassinations of Martin Luther King and Robert Kennedy; the Tet offensive; the violence of the 1968 Democratic convention in Chicago; the shootings at Kent State and Jackson State; the Weather Underground bombings; Watergate—that defined this tumultuous period of national life.

In reconstructing this history, Zuckerman does not diagnose the cause of the violence, but instead attempts to mirror the dizzying sense of unraveling that corresponds to how the Swede (and perhaps Zuckerman and even Roth) felt during the late 1960s.[15] Reading *American Pastoral*, it is easy to forget that much of what Zuckerman presents is his own fictional invention.[16] Although Zuckerman briefly encounters the Swede in the late 1980s, it is not until his forty-fifth high school reunion that he learns from the Swede's younger brother, Jerry, that Merry Levov has become the "Rimrock Bomber." Based on the limited facts he has of the Swede's life—the brief conversation he has with Jerry and a few newspaper clippings he can find on the bombing—Zuckerman goes about "dream[ing] a realistic chronicle" that not only would explain the Swede but also would illuminate the crumbling of America's postwar ascendancy in the late 1960s (89). Zuckerman's narrative expands from a psychological consideration of how the Swede would have reacted to this trauma—how he would have tried to assume responsibility for his daughter's actions—to a broader examination of the generational gulf that materialized in the late 1960s as the

Baby Boomer generation rebelled against the Vietnam War and the norms that had governed America's postwar expansion suddenly dissolved. While dancing with one of his high school classmates at the reunion, Zuckerman is "thinking of the Swede and of what happened to his country in a mere twenty-five years between the triumphant days at wartime Weequahic High and the explosion of his daughter's bomb in 1968, of that mysterious, troubling, extraordinary historical transition" (88).

Perhaps not surprisingly, considering his penchant for invention, Zuckerman does not begin his "realistic chronicle" with the known facts of the Swede's life. Instead, he starts with an invented scene where the ever-staid Levov loses his composure and ends up kissing the eleven-year-old Merry on the mouth, an in-explicable action triggered by the girl's constant stuttering (another Zuckerman invention). Both the stuttering and the kiss become useful metaphors for Zuck-erman's endeavors to understand "the sixties and . . . the disorder occasioned by the Vietnam War, of how certain families lost their kids and certain families didn't and how the Seymour Levovs were one of those that did—families full of tolerance and kindly, well-intentioned liberal goodwill, and theirs were the kids who went on a rampage, or went to jail, or disappeared underground, or fled to Sweden or Canada" (88). The stuttering, an affliction that has no known cause or resolution, embodies the inexplicable nature of Merry's actions and, more broadly, the disorder of the 1960s—the way so many upper-middle-class youth, emblemized by groups such as the Weather Underground, vehemently and violently rejected the triumphant narrative that the United States attempted to project after the Second World War. It is what Joan Didion in "Slouching To-wards Bethlehem," her 1967 exposé of San Francisco's hippie scene, describes as "the rules of the game we happened to be playing." "Maybe we had stopped believing in the rules ourselves, maybe we were having a failure of nerve about the game," Didion writes, suggesting how the chaos of the period, the sense of things falling apart, was difficult to comprehend.[17] As Robert Milder argues, "In portraying the radicalization of upper-middle-class youths, Zuckerman offers a variety of explanations without giving special weight to any of them. The rebellion may arise from generational conflict, exacerbated by the cultural divisions of the 1960s; from a flaw in the assimilationist ideal (Zuckerman offers Jewish Bucky Robinson as a foil to the Swede's self-styled Johnny Ap-pleseed); or, in Merry's case, from the confusion of being Jewish on one family side, Irish Catholic on another, as Lou Levov is convinced. It may be a protest against American capitalism, militarism, and racism (the views of Rita Cohen and Angela Davis), a rejection of the multi-generational American dream, or a response to the failure of America to extend that dream across the chasms of race and class."[18] For Roth, stuttering ultimately mirrors the illegibility of history, the ways in which disruptions like those that occurred during the 1960s can never be adequately diagnosed or anticipated.

The imagined kiss also offers an important clue for understanding how Zuckerman constructs the Swede's history.[19] In this imagined moment of passion between father and daughter, Roth anticipates the violence that is to come in the novel, while also highlighting the indeterminate and problematic nature of both history and authorship that remain essential to *American Pastoral* and the American Trilogy. In this sense, the kiss between father and daughter that marks Zuckerman's disappearance from the novel can be seen as his most crucial imaginative act, a fiction that Nathan invents as a potential, though inadequate, explanation for Merry Levov's uncontrollable fury. The impulse that informs his creation of this incident is, in many respects, transparent enough: the kiss is the moment Zuckerman needs to imagine the Swede not "as a god or a demigod in whose triumphs one could exult as a boy but his life as another assailable man" (89). More than just deflating his nostalgic memory of the Swede, the incestuous kiss gives Zuckerman and Roth's narrative its mythic heft, a symbolic shattering of American innocence that propels the Swede from his self-imagined Eden. RL Goldberg hypothesizes that this act of imagined incest would seem to be a rewriting of Milton's *Paradise Lost*, where Satan has an incestuous relationship with his daughter Sin, a relationship that results in the birth of Death. Goldberg contends that "simultaneous with national war, incest is the narrative rupture into which the anxieties of the domestic and the national collapse. Domestic and national sites—previously understood as interrelated but distinct—dissolve, revealing fault lines, fissures, and abortive hopes."[20] For just as the incestuous moment offers the Swede a tantalizing, if ultimately inadequate, explanation for his daughter's crimes, it similarly intimates how the violence of the 1960s can never be simply understood, either as a historical aberration or as a simple byproduct of a past generation's sins.

Although he clings to the idea that his breach caused his daughter's turn to violence, the Swede continually finds it to be an insufficient explanation for the bombing: "What went wrong with Merry? What did [the Swede] do to her that was so wrong? The kiss? That kiss? So beastly? How could a kiss make someone into a criminal? The aftermath of the kiss? The withdrawal? Was that the beastliness? But it wasn't as though he'd never held her or touched her or kissed her again—he *loved* her. She *knew* that" (92). In other words, what torments the Swede about his memory of the kiss is *not* that it offers him a simplified version of the past, one in which he can simply assume responsibility for his daughter's violence, but that it denies that simplified past while continuing to intimate that it could exist or *did* exist—his memory tantalizing him with the possibility that his actions *might or might not* have been responsible for

Merry's transformation. The memory then indicates the painful absence of the causality that the Swede desperately wants to believe in once again—his recollection of the incestuous moment teases him with a narrative that would not only explain Merry's actions but also allow him to assume responsibility for her violence. For while the kiss haunts him, his memory of it becomes a symptom of the tortured inner life that he experiences in the aftermath of the bombing, the explosion destroying the cohesive sense of self that he has always taken for granted. "Causes, clear answers, who there is to blame," the Swede thinks late in the novel. "Reasons. But there are no reasons. [Merry] is obliged to be as she is. We all are. Reasons are in books. Could how we lived as a family ever have come back as this bizarre horror? It couldn't. Jerry tries to rationalize it but you can't. This is all something else, something he knows absolutely nothing about. No one does. It is not rational. It is chaos. It is chaos from start to finish" (281).

The disorder exponentially escalates in the novel's concluding section, "Paradise Lost," as the Swede attempts to come to terms with all the chaos that has dissolved his sense of reality. Set during the summer of 1973, the summer of the Watergate hearings, "Paradise Lost" offers a portrait of a man and a nation ripped asunder. After looking for his daughter for five years, the Swede discovers her hiding out in the slums of Newark—a city utterly transformed by the 1967 riots—where she informs him that she has killed four more people, has been brutally raped, and as a result of these traumas has converted to Jainism. Now living in filth, she refuses to engage in the material world. Compounding his horror at his daughter's transformation, the Swede soon discovers that his wife, Dawn, is having an affair with their neighbor, Bill Orcutt, and that the Swede's former lover and Merry's former speech therapist, Sheila Salzman, harbored Merry in the days after the attack. "The old system that made order doesn't work anymore," Zuckerman writes in the novel's concluding pages. "All that was left was [the Swede's] fear and astonishment, but now concealed by nothing" (422).

Zuckerman charts the Swede's disintegration at a disastrous dinner party that he and Dawn host right after the Swede has reunited with Merry. At the party are the Swede's elderly parents visiting from Florida; the neighbor Bill Orcutt with his alcoholic wife, Jessie; Sheila and Shelly Salzman; and the Swede's high school friend turned Columbia law professor, Barry Umanoff, and his wife, Marcia, a literature professor and "militant nonconformist of staggering self-certainty," who celebrates all the chaos that seems to be occurring (339). The conversation soon turns to the Watergate hearings and *Deep Throat*, the 1972 pornographic film that enjoyed mainstream success. "The changes are beyond conception," the Swede's father, Lou, laments when debating the merits of *Deep Throat* with Marcia Umanoff. "I sometimes think that more has changed since 1945 than in all the years of history there have ever been. I don't know what to make of the end of so many things. The lack of feeling for individuals that a person sees in that movie, the lack of feeling for places like what is going on in Newark—how did this happen?" (365). Countering Lou's lament is Marcia Umanoff, who celebrates the liberating possibilities of transgression. "Without transgression there is no knowledge," the literature professor reminds the Swede's father. It is an argument that many of Roth's earlier protagonists (Alexander Portnoy, Mickey Sabbath, David Kepesh, the younger Nathan Zuckerman) have embraced. As Samuel Cohen argues, Marcia and Lou are essentially "rehearsing the central argument of Roth's fiction, and they are doing it in the end-of-the-1960s moment that gave it so much of its urgency."[21] In staging this scene, Zuckerman would seem to be upholding the necessity of rebellion—transgression is vital for revealing the disorderliness that constitutes both our personal and our political realities—while also recognizing and, to a certain extent, mourning all that is lost through such acts of rebellion.

For while many critics, perhaps most notably Norman Podhoretz, have read *American Pastoral* as Roth's great conservative rebuke of the 1960s, a sort of belated apology for the wrongs inflicted by *Portnoy's Complaint*, the novel ultimately resists such a reductive reading.[22] The novel's ambivalence toward the 1960s can be keenly felt in its closing as a drunken Jessie Orcutt almost blinds Lou with a fork after he has attempted to feed her some pie. At the near blinding, Marcia can only "laugh at their obtuseness to the flimsiness of the whole contraption, to laugh and laugh and laugh at them all, pillars of a society that, much to her delight, was going rapidly under" (423). The novel, however, does not seem to share Marcia's delight in "the assailability, the frailty, the enfeeblement of supposedly robust things" (423). In rethinking the unrest of the late 1960s, Zuckerman grants that there is no credible diagnosis for what triggered the violence that reshaped American life during that time. He would also seem to recognize that acts like Merry's bombing, and the vehemence of her anti-American rhetoric, uncovered the real and undiagnosable chaos that is a fundamental part of our personal and national lives while also affirming Lou Levov's lament that a certain "robustness" was lost during these years. "And what is wrong with their life," Zuckerman asks in the concluding sentences of the novel. "What on earth is less reprehensible than the life of the Levovs?" (423). The questions are both earnest and rhetorical: on the surface, the Swede's existence is exemplary, but his blindness to all the chaos that exists within life needs correction. Zuckerman, in the end, shows the Swede's need to assume responsibility for his daughter's actions as futile while also suggesting that the bombing uncovers the reality of American life, a reality that the Swede and his father have done their best to ignore. The fact that Zuckerman does not return to the present moment—when Nathan encountered his boyhood idol in 1995, the Swede was happily remarried with three sons—is equally important. The question of how the Swede and America more broadly are to resume their lives after the violence of the 1960s—after the reality of the "American berserk" has made its presence known—is one that Zuckerman refuses to answer. It is a question that haunts *American Pastoral* and that makes it one of Roth's most complex and substantial novels.

Published only a year after *American Pastoral*, *I Married a Communist* continues to explore how abruptly historical circumstances can overwhelm an individual person's life. Sharing a title with Howard Hughes's 1949 anti-Communist film (the film was quickly rechristened *The Woman on Pier 13* when the original name was panned by test audiences), *I Married a Communist* recovers the extreme political tenuousness of the early years of the Cold War, which was largely absent from Roth's earliest fiction.[23] Much the way he imagined the history of his boyhood idol in *American Pastoral*, Zuckerman turns his attention in *I Married a Communist* to two other figures from his Newark adolescence, Murray and Ira "Iron Rinn" Ringold. Murray was Nathan's beloved high school English teacher, while his younger brother Ira was a minor celebrity, a former ditch digger who transformed himself into a radio personality and outspoken political activist for leftist causes. While Murray offers a model of masculinity that the young Zuckerman finds inspiring, Ira is one of Roth's most compelling creations: a volatile and impassioned man whose inability to contain his proclivity for physical and rhetorical violence leads to his undoing. The novel hinges largely on how Ira's life is destroyed by his vindictive ex-wife, Eve Frame, a silent film star, who publishes a sensational memoir entitled *I Married a Communist* that outs Ringold as a member of the Communist party and falsely accuses him of being a spy for the Soviets. Due to his association with his brother, Murray is interrogated by the House Un-American Activities Committee, loses his job as a teacher, and is forced to work as a vacuum cleaner salesman for six years before regaining his former position.

I Married a Communist also continues the historiographic argument that *American Pastoral* explored. In telling Ira's story, Zuckerman preserves an account that has been lost to history while also making an argument that history can best be captured by the series of competing voices that Zuckerman has encountered throughout his lifetime. "But whatever the reason," Nathan concludes late in the novel, "the book of my life is a book of voices. When I ask myself how I arrived at where I am, the answer surprises me: 'Listening'" (222). This emphasis on "listening"—on capturing all the competing voices and contradictions that one encounters in a lifetime—remains central to the historiographic argument that Roth constructs in the American Trilogy, suggesting our notions of ourselves and of our nation can come into focus only once we allow in all the contradictions. Over the course of six summer evenings, Murray and Nathan replay the past, the older man filling in a history that Zuckerman, who left Newark behind him once he departed for the Army in 1954, has been unaware of. Their conversations force Zuckerman to reconsider his image of Iron Rinn—Murray reveals that his older brother killed a man when he was sixteen and that he was an adamant supporter of the Communist party—but also of this period of American life. The political unease of the HUAC years, the ways in which gossip and innuendo could abruptly undo a life, complicates Nathan's memories of the period; he even discovers that he was likely denied a Fulbright scholarship to study literature in Oxford due to the FBI's mistaken notion that Nathan was Ira's nephew (15).

Despite its rethinking of 1950s America, the novel was first read by many reviewers as being simply Roth's thinly veiled response to his ex-wife Claire Bloom's memoir, *Leaving a Doll's House* (1996). Bloom's book had painted Roth as a controlling and unstable partner, causing Roth a great deal of consternation. As Taylor reports, Roth maintained that his failure to win the Nobel Prize was due to the accusations made in Bloom's book, and he spent many of his retirement years writing "Notes for My Biographer" to attempt to refute her accusations.[24] Pierpont observes, "More than one reviewer had pointed out that Roth had done himself more damage than Bloom had, and that he had gone a good way toward proving her charges. The word 'misogynist' was back in common use, as even the most steadfast of Roth's admirers among female critics registered complaints."[25] The criticism of Roth's treatment of his female characters in *I Married a Communist* has merit: Eve Frame is one of Roth's least compelling creations, and Ira's downfall is too directly linked to Frame, her malicious memoir, and her daughter from a prior marriage, Sylphid. Even Ira's hatred of the ex-wife and the monstrous daughter, who convinces her mother to abort her child with Ira and whose presence leads to the dissolution of their marriage, is less vital than the all-consuming rage that propels Peter Tarnopol in *My Life as a Man*.

Yet to read *I Married a Communist* as solely Roth's revenge on Bloom unfairly ignores the more interesting questions the novel pursues. Along with *Operation Shylock*, in which he tackled the problem of Israel, *I Married a Communist* remains Roth's most politically engaged book as it explores the often-fraught intersection between politics and literature. Recalling one of his college literature professors, Leo Glucksman, a former GI turned academic, Zuckerman considers the tenuous relationship between literature and politics:

"Politics is the great generalizer," Leo told me, "and literature the great particularizer, and not only are they in an inverse relationship to each other—
they are in an *antagonistic* relationship. To politics, literature is decadent,
soft, irrelevant, boring, wrongheaded, dull, something that makes no sense
and that really oughtn't to be. Why? Because the particularizing impulse *is*
literature. How can you be an artist and renounce the nuance? But how can
you be a politician and *allow* the nuance? As an artist the nuance is your
task. Even should you choose to write in the simplest way, à la Hemingway,
the task remains to impart the nuance, to elucidate the contradiction, to
imply the contradiction. Not to erase the contradiction, not to deny the
contradiction, but to see where, within the contradiction, lies the tormented
human being. To allow for the chaos, to let it in. You *must* let it in. Otherwise you produce propaganda, if not for a political party, a political movement, then stupid propaganda for life itself—for life as it might itself prefer
to be publicized." (223)

Indeed, Glucksman's injunction against political fiction would "seem as close
to a credo as Roth has ever written."[26] On the one hand, this argument against
political fiction—a clear reaction against the leftist and social realist fiction of
the 1930s—would seem to be a product of the style of literary Modernism that
was very much in vogue when Roth launched his career. An aversion to politics
can be felt throughout much of his early fiction; the stories in *Goodbye, Columbus* would seem to be products of the sort of fictional aesthetics for which
Glucksman advocates. Glucksman's insistence on literature's ability to be "the
great particularizer" reflects Roth's methodology throughout the American
Trilogy as he meticulously captures the particulars of experience and refuses
to resolve the contradictions that torment his protagonists' sense of themselves
and their nation. That said, Roth would also seem to be correcting his earlier
fiction, where politics and history were largely muted, suggesting literature can
engage with the particulars of politics and fiction without succumbing to a
simplified political position.

Beyond reflecting on the political capacities of fiction, *I Married a Communist* also traces the history of the American Left and of progressive politics
in the second half of the twentieth century. The novel chronicles the Left's slow
decline in the fifty years following the Second World War. Even Murray Ringold, who as an educator championed the teachers' union, laments the demise
of the union's purpose: "Now the union is a big disappointment to me. Just
become a money-grubbing organization. Pay, that's all. What to do to educate
the kids is the last thing on anybody's mind. Big disappointment" (14). The

same verdict could also be reached for the nation at large. As Zuckerman—who has retired from public (and sexual) life and lives in near seclusion in the Berkshires—surveys America at the end of the century, a creeping nihilism grips his imagination. At the end of the novel, Murray reveals that his wife, Doris, was killed in a mugging in Newark when "somebody cracked her skull open with a brick" for her empty handbag (317). The waste inherent in Doris's death, a murder that Murray blames on his own reluctance to abandon Newark, inspires Zuckerman's concluding verdict on American life: "We could have sat on my deck for six hundred nights before I heard the entire story of how Murray Ringold, who'd chosen to be nothing more extraordinary than a high school teacher, had failed to elude the turmoil of his time and place and ended up no less a historical casualty than his brother" (318). Zuckerman's insistence that we are all "casualities" of history is an argument that Roth repeats throughout the American Trilogy and reinforces in his later fiction, *The Plot Against America* and the Nemeses tetralogy.

I Married a Communist concludes with one of Roth's most moving passages as Zuckerman recalls a story his mother told him after his grandfather's death, about how the deceased are transformed into stars. "What you see from this silent rostrum up on my mountain on a night as splendidly clear as that night Murray left me for good—for the very best of loyal brothers, the ace of English teachers, died in Phoenix two months later—is that universe into which error does not obtrude. You see the inconceivable: the colossal spectacle of no antagonism. You see with your eyes the vast brain of time, a galaxy of fire set by no human hand" (323). The nihilism that Zuckerman flirts with here is countered only by the spectacle of the night sky, the sense not only that death releases us from the conflicts that define our personal and national histories, but that there somehow exists a galaxy free of such turmoil.

While *I Married a Communist* received mixed reviews, *The Human Stain* would return Roth to critical favor and bring the American Trilogy to a satisfying conclusion. *The Human Stain* forcefully returns to the questions of identity formation that Roth asked in *Goodbye, Columbus*, but with a much greater awareness of how the circumstances of history can undo even the boldest acts of self-definition. At the heart of the novel is Coleman "Silky" Silk, a light-skinned African American star student and amateur boxer from East Orange, New Jersey, who decides upon entering the Navy during the Second World War to pass as a Jew. Over the course of his life, Silk relishes his secret as he thrives in his self-fashioned existence as a Jewish man. He constructs his life as an elaborate performance, marrying a Jewish woman, Iris, and raising three children while also climbing the academic ranks, becoming a renowned classics professor and then the dean of faculty at Athena College.

Silk's existence, however, falls apart when he is accused of racism by two African American students after he calls them "spooks" for never attending his class. While Silk was referring to ghosts, the students claim that he used it as a racial epithet, and when Silk refuses to apologize he ends up resigning his position. "Spooks! To be undone by a word that no one even speaks anymore," Zuckerman writes late in the novel. "To hang him on that was, for Coleman, to banalize everything—the elaborate clockwork of his lie, the beautiful calibration of his deceit, *everything*" (334–5). Silk becomes undone by his rage, blaming his wife's death on how his colleagues failed to support him. He regains his equilibrium only when he starts an affair with the much younger Faunia Farley, an illiterate janitor at Athena, a relationship that outrages not only Silk's children and Faunia's ex-husband Lester, an embittered Vietnam veteran who eventually murders Silk and Faunia by forcing their car off the road, but also the Athena community. It is only after Silk's death that his reputation can be restored—at his funeral, one of his colleagues lauds him as a great "American individualist" continuing the tradition of "Hawthorne, Melville, and Thoreau" (310). Yet, the colleague remains unaware of Silk's actual identity, which remains a secret to all but Zuckerman, who learns the truth from Silk's estranged sister, Ernestine, who quietly attends her brother's funeral.

Like *American Pastoral*, where he had few facts upon which to base his narrative reconstruction of the Swede, Zuckerman has limited access to his subject's actual story: Zuckerman bases his narrative on the few facts that Ernestine gives him, an aborted interview with Faunia's estranged father, and the local sheriff (and Faunia's former lover) who denies the rumors that Coleman drove off the road because Faunia was performing oral sex on him. In reimagining Silk's life, Zuckerman emphasizes acts of reading and misreading—in a crucial early scene, Zuckerman has Silk misread a poem that his white lover, Steena, has written him, mistaking the word "neck" for "negro" (112). Such moments of misreading are central to *The Human Stain*, as the novel illustrates how easily language can obscure the truth, how words (and people) can be misread. To be alive is to misread and misinterpret; the true story always remains painfully elusive. By putting such an emphasis on reading and performance, on the instability of language and all the harm that a single word can occasion, *The Human Stain*, as Ross Posnock contends, "asks its readers to be game, invites them to tap their own capacity for interpretive play."[27]

Even more than this emphasis on reading, *The Human Stain* displays Zuckerman's capacity for imagining the lives of others, as his narrative not only reconstructs Silk, but also has sections devoted to Faunia, Lester, and Delphine Roux, Coleman's colleague at Athena who pushes for his ouster yet harbors a romantic crush on him. The sections of the novel where Zuckerman ventures out to imagine these other perspectives—with the exception of Delphine's perspective, which feels a bit cartoonish compared to the others—differentiate *The Human Stain* from its predecessors in the trilogy as Zuckerman expands his fictional range, suggesting his ability to render emotionally credible characters. Indeed, the sections narrated from Faunia's perspective are among the novel's most engaging, and she remains, with *Sabbath Theater*'s Drenka Balich, one of Roth's fully formed female characters. A victim of sexual abuse whose children are killed in a housefire, Faunia Farley is one of Roth's most tragic characters, yet Zuckerman gives her a rich interior life and imagination that shatter the community's notions of her as an illiterate janitor.

Throughout the novel, Roth also interrogates our desire for purity, for the unyielding promise of innocence that the pastoral portends. "Ninety-eight in New England was a summer of exquisite warmth and sunshine, in baseball a summer of mythical battle between a home-run god who was white [Mark McGwire] and a home-run god who was brown [Sammy Sosa]," Zuckerman muses in the novel's opening pages, "and in America the summer of an enormous piety binge, a purity binge, when terrorism—which had replaced communism as the prevailing threat to the country's security—was succeeded by cocksucking, and a virile, youthful middle-aged president and a brash, smitten twenty-one-year-old employee carrying on in the Oval Office like two teenage kids in a parking lot revived America's oldest communal passions, historically perhaps its most treacherous and subversive pleasure: the ecstasy of sanctimony" (2). The novel links the Clinton scandal with Coleman's seemingly inappropriate relationship with Faunia, both affairs subject to the American puritanical impulse to condemn—what Zuckerman diagnoses as the "tyranny of propriety" (153). Counter to this tradition that emphasizes the need for purity, a purity that can never be attained, Zuckerman posits the importance of the *stain* as a vital part of human experience. Recalling a crow abandoned by its compatriots because it was touched by human hands, Faunia continues the novel's critique of purity while also arguing for the vitality of the "human stain." Zuckerman writes:

> *That's how it is*—in her own dry way, that is all Faunia was telling the girl feeding the snake: we leave a stain, we leave a trail, we leave our imprint. Impurity, cruelty, abuse, error, excrement, semen—there's no other way to be here. Nothing to do with grace or salvation or redemption. It's in everyone. Indwelling. Inherent. Defining. That stain that is there before its mark. Without the sign it is there. The stain so intrinsic it doesn't require a mark. The stain that *precedes* disobedience, that *encompasses* disobedience and perplexes all explanation and understanding. It's why all the cleansing is a

joke. A barbaric joke at that. The fantasy of purity is appalling. It's insane. What is the quest to purify, if not *more* impurity? All she was saying about the stain was that it's inescapable. That, naturally, would be Faunia's take on it: the inevitably stained creatures that we are. (242)

Highlighting this moment, Aimee Pozorski argues that Faunia's musings become "a religion of the stain, of impurity; by reversing the common religious notion that human beings come into the world pure, Zuckerman imagines that Faunia locates a commonality between the Greeks of *The Iliad* and the American people of the 1990s: the only 'way to be here' is to leave our human stink, our stain, on others."[28] On the one hand, Faunia's musings connect her to Mickey Sabbath; both embrace the essential messiness, the rage and the passion, of human experience. Not surprisingly, Faunia rejects the "infinitely alone" Hebrew God and "the desexualized Christian man-god and his uncontaminated mother," instead adopting a view of divinity that reflects the chaos of existence (243). The novel ultimately indicts America's particular need to moralize and desexualize experience—the community's fascination and outrage over the Clinton scandal and Coleman's affair with Faunia would seem, for Zuckerman, to be a byproduct of the nation's Puritan past—while also insisting on the madness, the violence and sexual energy that exist beneath the veneer of American life.

Not surprisingly, Roth returns to the image of the false pastoral to conclude the trilogy. *The Human Stain* ends with Zuckerman confronting Faunia's ex-husband, Lester, while the embittered Vietnam veteran is fishing in the Berkshires. "Just facing him," Zuckerman writes in the novel's concluding paragraph, "I could feel the terror of the auger—even with him already seated on his bucket: the icy white of the lake encircling a tiny spot that was a man, the only human marker in all of nature, like the X of an illiterate's signature on a sheet of paper. There it was, if not the whole story, the whole picture. Only rarely, at the end of our century, does life offer up a vision as pure and peaceful as this one: a lake that's constantly turning over its water atop an arcadian mountain in America" (360–1). This closing image—the peaceful, mountain waters veiling the actuality of American life—perfectly captures the argument that Zuckerman and Roth have pursued throughout the American Trilogy, the three novels illustrating how America's mythic sense of itself, seen in the pastoral innocence that the bucolic Berkshires setting projects, conceals a more complicated and inscrutable reality. That Zuckerman compares the image of Lester to "the X of an illiterate's signature" is also fitting, as it returns to the novel's engagement with acts of reading. But, as Zuckerman realizes, efforts to interpret the meaning of the "X"—whether it be someone's past or a national history—are bound to be wrong. Yet, the thousand-plus pages of the American Trilogy are not a pessimistic assessment of our ability to understand the past or the problem of "other people," but instead a reflection on the human need to make narrative sense of ourselves and our national experience. In the end, rather than diagnose the meaning behind the United States' postwar experience, Roth captures the maddening contradictions, the violence that exists within the pastoral dream, that runs through the nation's history.

CHAPTER 7

Late Works

The Plot Against America and the Nemeses Tetralogy

Delivering the 2018 Philip Roth Lecture, Salman Rushdie described Roth, who had died that May of heart failure at the age of eighty-five, as a "political prophet" for the way his final novels had anticipated the political turmoil of American life in the twenty-first century. Roth's late work largely continues the themes that he had pursued in the American Trilogy, but with a heightened awareness of how fragile our national and personal good fortunes are. At an age when many novelists retire or slow down, Roth remained creatively viable and prolific in his seventies, publishing six novels in his seventh decade before announcing his retirement from writing fiction in 2012. This chapter will focus on Roth's major late works, *The Plot Against America* (2004) and the Nemeses tetralogy (*Everyman* [2006], *Indignation* [2008], *The Humbling* [2009], and *Nemesis* [2010]).[1] From the violence of the Korean War captured in *Indignation* to the horrors of an imagined polio outbreak in *Nemesis*, Roth's final novels underscore the fragile nature of our existence. "History claims everybody," Roth declared in his 2004 essay "My Uchronia," and it's this maxim that underpins his late fiction (*Why Write?* 344).[2] While the American Trilogy was more concerned with historiographic concerns—how our knowledge of the past is always shaped by the constraints of narrative—*The Plot Against America* and the Nemeses tetralogy demonstrate the blunt power of history, how shifting and unexpected historical circumstances can suddenly and dramatically alter our lives. The sense of alarm that Roth registers in "My Uchronia," an alarm triggered by the United States' invasion of Afghanistan and Iraq in the early 2000s, reflects the uncertain tenor that runs throughout the fiction he published in the new century. Defining the notion of history that emerges in Roth's later work, Michael Kimmage observes that, for Roth, "we are less the authors of history than history—in its Tolstoyan waves of chaos—is the author of our fate, the capricious master of our destiny, able to destroy and scatter and disperse, to cause suffering when it wishes and to leave injustice as mere injustice, unredeemed."[3]

History becomes an active, all-consuming force in Roth's late works as his protagonists often appear helpless against the circumstances imposed upon them through their historical moment. Most spectacularly, in *The Plot Against America* Roth reimagines his own childhood if the United States had veered toward the anti-Semitism that engulfed Europe during the Second World War. Roth revisits his formative years, respectively, in *Indignation* and *Nemesis*. In the former, Roth reflects on how the realities of the Korean War—a conflict that by happenstance of age Roth was able to avoid narrowly—destroy the life of the young Marcus Messner, who is killed in action. In *Nemesis*, history comes in the form of an imagined polio outbreak that decimates Newark's children during the summer of 1944. The losses are more private in the other two entries of the Nemeses tetralogy—in *Everyman*, Roth chronicles the deterioration of the human body while in *The Humbling* he captures what happens to an aging actor who suddenly loses his ability to perform—but they continue the emphasis on how unexpected events and losses can transform a life. Roth suggests the tetralogy's "pathos is grounded in the innocence of people when they are truly up against it, when the greatest emergency imaginable arises and existence becomes an inexplicable problem they cannot solve. All accustomed safeguards vanish, abruptly nothing is on one's side, and, however impregnable one may have once seemed, however gifted, determined, decisive, however rectitudinous, disaster ensues—and nothing is more real" (*Why Write?* 385).

The insidious nature of history, however, emerges most fully in *The Plot Against America*, Roth's counterfactual novel in which Charles Lindbergh defeats Franklin Roosevelt in the 1940 presidential election. First released in the months leading up to the 2004 presidential election, *The Plot Against America* remains the most substantial and ambitious of the novels that Roth published in the wake of the American Trilogy. By presenting a credible alternate history where the United States under a President Lindbergh signs a non-aggression pact with Nazi Germany, *The Plot Against America* reveals that "*all the assurances are provisional*, even here in a two-hundred-year-old democracy" (*Why Write?* 344–5). "We are ambushed," Roth writes in "My Uchronia," "even as free Americans in a powerful republic armed to the teeth, by the unpredictability that is history" (*Why Write?* 345). While some critics have read the novel as a roman à clef response to George W. Bush's first term as president, in particular to his administration's restrictions on civil liberties that occurred in the wake of the September 11th terrorist attacks, *The Plot Against America* is not primarily an indictment of any particular president or political party. The novel instead exposes the tenuous nature of American democracy.[4] "Fear presides over these memories, a perpetual fear," Roth writes in the novel's opening sentence, suggesting the trauma of the Lindbergh presidency has not only dissolved the secure world of his childhood but also lingered with him throughout his adult life (1). In the opening chapter of *The Facts*, Roth recalls that while he "never doubted that this country was mine (and New Jersey and Newark as well), I was not unaware of the power to intimidate that emanated from the highest and lowest reaches of gentile America" (20). He goes on to describe the "'race riots,' as we children called the hostile nighttime invasions by the boys from Neptune [New Jersey]" at nearby Bradley Beach, a Jersey Shore vacation spot popular among Jews: "violence directed against the Jews by youngsters who, as everyone said, could only have learned their hatred from what they heard at home" (*The Facts* 24).

The fear that was only a minor note of Roth's childhood becomes the predominant theme in *The Plot Against America* as he imagines what would have happened if the security offered by his family and the Jewish community in Weequahic had been shattered by a president who enflamed anti-Semitic sentiments. In Lindbergh, Roth located a figure who could have credibly defeated Roosevelt in the 1940 presidential election by playing on isolationist sentiment. "It turned out," Roth writes in the aftermath of Lindbergh's overwhelming electoral victory, "the experts concluded, that twentieth-century Americans, weary of confronting a new crisis in every decade, were starving for normalcy, and what Charles A. Lindbergh represented was normalcy raised to heroic proportions, a decent man with an honest face and undistinguished voice who had resoundingly demonstrated to the entire planet the courage to take charge and the fortitude to shape history and, of course, the power to transcend personal tragedy" (53). After signing the non-aggression pact with Nazi Germany, Lindbergh initiates a series of programs meant to marginalize Jewish Americans—initiating the Office of American Absorption, formed ostensibly to aid Jewish Americans in assimilating into "mainstream" American life, but in reality meant to dissolve predominately Jewish neighborhoods and enclaves. Until Lindbergh mysteriously disappears in the novel's final movement, an event that triggers mass riots and allows Roosevelt to reclaim the White House, *The Plot Against America* does not swerve into the outlandish; Roth's depiction of the Lindbergh administration remains grounded in Lindbergh's actual public utterances. Indeed, the novel's postscript, which carefully recounts the actual histories of the novel's main figures, suggests Roth's desire to keep his counterhistory grounded in reality.

At the heart of the novel is Roth's attempt to conserve his memories of his family and of the Newark that he relished as a child. Of all his novels, *The Plot Against America* remains the most grounded in Roth's memories of growing up in the Weequahic section of Newark as the beloved younger son of Herman and Bess Roth, and in many ways the novel offers the fullest and most affectionate portrait of Roth's family life. "I wanted to imagine my childhood exactly as it was," Roth notes in *Here We Are*, "Herman, Bess, Sandy [Roth's older brother], me—but take away the Rooseveltian certitudes so as to steep us in the dark times of a Lindbergh, 'America First' presidency."[5] Perhaps not surprisingly, Roth devotes the novel's opening pages to reconstructing the details of his Newark childhood and of the Weequahic neighborhood that shaped his sense of the world. "We were a happy family in 1940," Roth writes in the novel's opening pages. "My parents were outgoing, hospitable people, their friends culled from among my father's associates at the office and from the women who along with mother had helped to organize the Parent-Teacher Association at newly built Chancellor Avenue School, where my brother and I were pupils. All were Jews" (2). Andy Connolly observes, "The Roth household [in the novel] is thus run along prudent and yet warmly loving lines that reflect what so many historians have discussed as the abiding promise of security wrought by the New Deal's rational schemes for delivering American citizens from the instabilities and fears that had so gravely beset the nation following the onset of the Great Depression."[6] Ultimately, *The Plot Against America* traces what happens when that sense of security—a security that springs from both the stability provided by parents and from the promises of American democracy—suddenly falls away. In doing this, Roth imagines what would have happened if the bedrock of his artistic life and political faith had been irreparably damaged in his childhood. Indeed, Roth's image of himself as an American writer was largely founded on the patriotism that had been instilled in him as a child during the Depression and the Second World War, and *The Plot Against America* asks what would have happened if that faith had been punctured during Roth's formative years.

Narrated largely from the perspective of a seven-year-old Philip Roth, the novel focuses on the child's terror as he realizes that all the larger institutions meant to shield him—his nation, his schools, his family—cannot protect him from the larger realities of the political world. In his 1988 interview with the Israeli novelist Aharon Appelfeld, a survivor of the Holocaust, Roth mentions the usefulness of employing "the viewpoint of a child, who has no historical calendar in which to place unfolding events and no intellectual means of penetrating their meaning" when attempting to fictionalize the horrors of the Holocaust, as Appelfeld had done in his novel *The Age of Wonders* (1978), a notion that

Roth embraces in *The Plot Against America* (*Why Write?* 205). In depicting life under Lindbergh, the fictional Philip focuses less on the national consequences of the new president's policies than on how the terror Lindbergh represents unravels his family. "A new life began for me," Roth writes after his cousin, Alvin, has returned home after losing his leg in the Second World War (he enlists through the Canadian military). "I'd watched my father fall apart, and I would never return to the same childhood. The mother at home was now away all day working for Hahne's, the brother on call was now off after school working for Lindbergh, and the father who'd defiantly serenaded all those callow cafeteria anti-Semites in Washington was crying aloud with his mouth wide open—crying like both a baby abandoned and a man being tortured—because he was powerless to stop the unforeseen. And as Lindbergh's election couldn't have made clearer to me, the unfolding of the unforeseen was everything" (113).

The trauma of this moment—Philip's vigorous father reduced to an open wound—is at the heart of the novel's argument, illustrating how politics and "unforeseen" historical developments can shatter one's daily existence. As Claudia Roth Pierpont observes, history in the novel appears "not as a grand epic but as the chaos and disaster that ordinary people go through." She continues, "The book is also clearly responsive to Roth's sore awareness of having grown up safe in America, at a time when Jewish children in Europe were suffering and dying, an awareness that runs from his earlies stories right through *The Ghost Writer*."[7] At the conclusion of the novel, Roth affirms the ways in which the trauma of the Lindbergh years has lingered with him throughout his adult life. "But then it was over. The nightmare was over," Roth writes in the novel's penultimate chapter. "Lindbergh was gone and we were safe, though never would I be able to revive that unfazed sense of security first fostered in a little child by a big, protective republic and his ferociously responsible parents" (301). Roth's linking of his parents and his nation here is significant. For Roth, the promises of American democracy—the freedom to pursue one's own identity and happiness—remain tethered to the child's sense of security that he internalized from his parents and the comforting moral certainty projected by Roosevelt during the Depression and the Second World War.

The Plot Against America, however, restores the history that the Lindbergh presidency has driven off course, a move that complicates the historical argument that Roth pursues throughout the novel. Once Lindbergh mysteriously disappears in a flight from Louisville back to Washington, DC, history quickly restores itself: a special election returns Roosevelt to the White House, the Japanese bomb Pearl Harbor (a year late), the United States enters the Second World War, and history resumes its normal course. Late in the novel, after the journalist Walter Winchell has been murdered in the wake of announcing his presidential candidacy, Roth is careful to mention that Robert F. Kennedy is assassinated on June 14, 1968, a detail that suggests that the Lindbergh presidency has had no overarching effect on postwar American history (*Plot* 272).[8] Timothy Parrish has argued that the reversion of history in the book's conclusion ends up "reinforcing an idealized view of America as the last, best place in which one may pursue the seemingly endless opportunities for self-reinvention and renewal."[9] Parrish's reading of the novel's conclusion has merit: *The Plot Against America* quickly restores history to its proper order, and it does not interrogate the forces within American life that enabled Lindbergh to get elected. Like the dream the fictional Philip Roth has in the novel where his beloved stamps of America's National Parks have been overwritten with a black swastika, an image reinforcing the notion that evil is being imprinted upon the nation rather than emerging from it, the novel's conclusion suggests that what threatens American life is some external force (43).

Nevertheless, *The Plot Against America* ends by reaffirming the lasting trauma imposed by the Lindbergh years. While history continues its normal course, the narrative intimates that the fear and guilt of those years lingered with the fictional Philip throughout his adult life, a fear that irreversibly reorients his sense of himself and his nation. Not surprisingly, the novel ends by stressing Philp's lasting guilt for his own participation in the Lindbergh nightmare. For it is ultimately Philip's actions that haunt him: earlier in the novel, he attempts to convince his Aunt Evelyn to prevent his family's forced relocation to Danville, Kentucky (where they have been ordered to move under the newly instated Homestead Act 42, which relocates Jewish families to more rural parts of America), and he even suggests that his neighbor, Seldon Wishnow, a boy whom Philip does not like, be sent in his place. Philip's action triggers the Wishnow family's relocation to rural Kentucky, where Seldon's mother is murdered by members of the Klu Klux Klan. At the end of the novel, the orphaned Seldon becomes the embodiment of the ill-fitting "stump" that Roth's cousin Alvin was fitted with after losing his leg in combat. "There was no stump for me to care for this time," Roth declares in the novel's concluding sentences. "The boy himself was the stump, and until [Seldon] was taken to live with his mother's married sister in Brooklyn ten months later, I was the prosthesis" (362). The closing image of the novel—the orphaned Seldon transformed into the open wound caused by the Lindbergh presidency—captures how such historical traumas can never be adequately treated. The pain of the phantom limb, the sense of security that Lindbergh ripped away, remains keenly felt even decades after the trauma. Such trauma can, perhaps, be narrated, but it can never be fully resolved or healed. The quickness with which our historical circumstances can shift and utterly overwhelm us—even in a nation as seemingly protected as the United States—would seem to be the central lesson that Roth imparts in the novel. It's perhaps not surprising that the novel gained resonance during the Trump years as the nation, to many of its citizens, seemed to drift toward the violence and discrimination depicted in the novel, an association reinforced by David Simon and Ed Burn's adaptation of *The Plot Against America* that premiered on HBO in 2020.

The emphasis on the "relentless unforeseen" that drives *The Plot Against America* becomes the cornerstone of the Nemeses tetralogy, the slender four novels that cap off Roth's half-century career. Toward the conclusion of *Everyman*, the first entry in the tetralogy, the anonymous protagonist, who has spent the night telephoning ailing former colleagues and friends, wishes that he could once again talk to his long-deceased mother and father about the unimaginable losses that occur with age. "Yet what he'd learned was nothing when measured against the inevitable onslaught that is the end of life," Roth writes of his everyman. "Had he been aware of the moral suffering of every man and woman he happened to have known during all his years of professional life, of each one's painful story of regret and stoicism, of fear and panic and isolation and dread, had he learned of every last thing they had parted with that had once been vitally theirs and of how, systematically, they were being destroyed, he had would have had to stay on the phone through the day and into the night, making another hundred calls at least. Old age isn't a battle; old age is a massacre" (155–6). Such moments reflect the grim tenor and obsession with death that characterizes Roth's final books and more broadly suggest how the Nemeses sequence reflects—both in style and in subject matter—the devastating realities of aging and the failings of the human body. The tetralogy exposes the alienation central to how Roth imagined his status as a writer of his age and his experience at that moment in American history, as the nation struggled to respond to the uncertainties and challenges of the new millennium.

Early in *The Humbling*, the third novel of the sequence, Jerry Oppenheim (the agent for the novel's protagonist, the diminished actor Simon Axler) attempts to convince Simon to resume his career after he has suffered a devastating and mysterious crisis in confidence, his talent and capacity for performing having seemingly vanished overnight. "Let's face it, there's a panic that comes with age," the agent tells his client. "I'm that much older than you, and I've been dealing with it for years [. . .] So you start to feel afraid, to feel soft, to feel that you don't have that raw live power anymore. It scares you. With the result, as you say, that you're not free anymore. There's nothing happening—and that's terrifying" (35–6). The sense of diminishment that Oppenheim expresses here pervades the tetralogy, a grouping that Roth made only upon the publication of *Nemesis* in 2010. In their brevity, these four works would seem to be deliberately and self-consciously minor, as if Roth were responding to the limitations—the depletion and the sense of fragmentation—that frequently impose themselves on the aging artist. In his review of *Nemesis*, J. M. Coetzee reaches a similar conclusion, arguing that Roth's final works have been "composed, as it were, in a minor key. One can read them with admiration for their craft, their intelligence, their seriousness; but nowhere does one feel that the creative flame is burning at white heat, or the author being stretched by his material."[10]

Coetzee's assessment seems only partially accurate: the "minor" quality of these works should be viewed as quite purposeful, as if Roth were self-consciously stripping his work so that all that remains are its most essential elements. The sparseness of these novels would seem to be integral to their design. The sense of play, the exhaustive (and exhausting) competing voices that have characterized much of Roth's fiction are largely absent, having been replaced with an almost steely-eyed narrative sensibility that seems fixed on narrating just the basics of the story. Events (mostly catastrophes) within these novels occur with little sense of causation: whether they are large crises such as a polio outbreak, the onslaught of the Korean War, or private mysteries, there is no exploration of why—why one's health fails, why the capacity for acting just evaporates—things *just happen* within these novels. Throughout the tetralogy, Roth resists providing the fictive tissue that novels typically offer. "He was imagining the least likely thing that might happen, which was why he was imagining it," Roth writes of Simon Axler's sudden desire to father a child with his much younger lover, Pegeen Stapleford, in *The Humbling*, a development that is typical of the narrative swerves these novels take (116). Indeed, a sense of incompleteness and alienation haunts Roth's final novels, with the implicit argument being that such feelings, as disturbing and unsatisfying as they may be, are integral to the aging artist's experience. "The power of subjectivity in the late works of art is the irascible gesture with which it takes leave of the works themselves," Theodor Adorno observed in his consideration of Beethoven's late symphonies. "Of the works themselves it leaves only fragments behind, and communicates itself, like a cipher, only through the blank spaces from which it has disengaged itself. Touched by death, the hand of the master sets free the masses of material he used to form; its tears and fissures, witnesses to the finite powerlessness of the I confronted with Being, are its final work" (566).[11]

These "tears and fissures" permeate Roth's twenty-first-century fiction. In its deliberate difficulty, the Nemeses tetralogy grapples with the formal and political implications that Edward Said and Adorno theorize in their notions of late style. In *On Late Style*, Said asserts: "Late style is *in*, but oddly *apart* from the present. Only certain artists and thinkers care enough about their métier to believe that it too ages and must face death and failing senses and memory."[12] Alongside Don DeLillo and Toni Morrison's slim late novels, the Nemeses books would seem to be a deliberate and highly self-conscious exercise in late style, as Roth considers the aesthetic and political implications of late style as a novelist deliberately approaching the end of his career. Reflecting on the reduced scope of his final novels, Roth, citing Bellow and Conrad's novellas as inspiration, commented: "I felt I'd gone as far as I could with amplification. It was time to turn to compression, to brevity, instead. To go back to where I'd begun, but knowing things the bright young comedian of *Goodbye, Columbus* couldn't know."[13] Taken together, the four Nemeses novels signal an artistic imagination that is not so much exhausted, but one that is, rather self-consciously, attempting to reflect the sense of alienation, an estrangement both artistic and cultural, which Roth saw as being essential to his writerly identity at the end of his career.

In many respects, *Everyman*, the opening novel of the tetralogy, remains representative of the approach and tenor that characterize the series. Taking its title from a fifteenth-century allegorical play, *Everyman* starts with the burial of the anonymous protagonist, a thrice-married retired commercial artist who dies while undergoing a heart procedure, and then looks back to trace the many ailments he has to endure during his life—a childhood hernia, appendicitis in midlife, and finally the various heart ailments that plague him in final decades. Despite its title, *Everyman* is not so much an allegory—and in interviews Roth emphatically states as much—as a history of the failing human body, and Roth meticulously renders the details of his protagonist's many physical ailments.[14] Despite the robust picture of Roth featured on the first edition of the novel, *Everyman* reflects Roth's firsthand experience with pain and illness. Ira Nadel reports that Roth first suffered a back injury when he was in the Army in 1954; he would suffer a burst appendix in 1967, and later he would have extensive heart problems, resulting in a quintuple bypass surgery in 1989.[15] That being said, history does eventually intrude into what, on first reading, seems like novel not interested in history. The first intrusion can be felt early in the book as Roth's anonymous protagonist prepares for hernia surgery, a procedure that, as a child, he is afraid will either kill him or leave him emasculated. On the eve of his surgery, "at first he didn't fall asleep because of his waiting for the boy [in the bed next to him] to die, and then he didn't because he couldn't stop thinking of the drowned body that had washed up on the beach that past summer. It was the body of a seaman whose tanker had been torpedoed by a German U-boat. The Coast Guard beach patrol had found the body amid the oil scum and shattered cargo cases at the edge of the beach that was only a block away from the house where his family of four rented a room for each summer. . . .

The war was closer than most people imagined, and so was the horror" (25–6). This moment neatly encapsulates the historical argument that Roth explores in *Indignation* and *Nemesis* (as well as *The Plot Against America* and *American Pastoral*)—that the "horror" of history is always much closer than we would like to imagine. Yet, the inflection of this scene feels quite different from what we get in those aforementioned "historical" novels—the horror of history does not pull Roth's everyman down but instead reflects the existential terror that the boy acutely feels before his surgery. Later in the novel, history—in the form of large-scale catastrophe—once again reemerges as Roth's anonymous protagonist considers the aftermath of the September 11th terrorist attacks on his sense of himself. Soon after he is rebuffed (or "ghosted") by a young woman he watches running on the shore, a failure that sends him reeling, he considers moving back Manhattan to be closer to his daughter Nancy, the one child with whom he has a meaningful relationship. "Even before 9/11," Roth writes, "he had contemplated a retirement of the kind he'd been living for three years now; the disaster of 9/11 had appeared to accelerate his opportunity to make a big change, when in fact it had marked the beginning of his vulnerability and the origin of his exile" (135). The scenario that Roth's everyman considers is one that Nathan Zuckerman attempted in *Exit Ghost*. Yet, *Everyman*'s anonymous protagonist fails to make the leap that Zuckerman attempts in that novel; he retreats into seclusion after hearing his second wife (and Nancy's mother) has had a debilitating stroke.

What's striking here is that history—in the form of 9/11—becomes a metaphor for the devastation that Roth's everyman feels as an integral part of his experience of aging, the enormous loss that surrounds the physical body's deterioration (and seeing one's friends and lovers suffer a similar fate). Historical events don't trigger the losses—as they will later will in *Indignation* and *Nemesis*—but instead they become a way through which those wounds can be understood. While Roth's protagonist in some ways imagines the catastrophic loss of 9/11 has shaped his impulses, the event becomes for him a metaphor through which he can view his own circumstances. And instead of being pulled into history, the novel's protagonist finds himself being cut free from it into the oblivion of death: "But now it appeared that like any number of the elderly, he was in the process of becoming less and less and would have to see his aimless day through to the end as no more than what he was—the aimless days and the uncertain nights and the impotently putting up with the physical deterioration and the terminal sadness and the waiting and waiting for nothing" (161).

History returns to the forefront in Roth's next novel, *Indignation*. Set during the height of the Korean War, the novel focuses on Marcus Messner, a college sophomore who, despite his father's great anxiety that his son's life is in grave danger, gets expelled from college for not attending the school's required chapel services. Marcus's expulsion results in him getting drafted into the Army, where he is shipped to the frontlines of the war and is quickly killed in action, suffering a gruesome death on what would later become known as Massacre Mountain. The novel revisits the terrain that Roth explored in his earliest fiction: Marcus's experience at the fictional Winesburg College would seem to be loosely based on Roth's own tenure at Bucknell College, an experience that Roth narrates in the "Joe College" section of his memoir, *The Facts*.[16] While Roth was able to escape unscathed by history at his time in Bucknell, which is located in the small town of Lewisburg, Pennsylvania, Marcus Messner, who shares the young Roth's disdain for religion and for sanctimony, is not so lucky. "Yes, the good old defiant American 'Fuck you,' and that was it for the butcher's son, dead three months short of his twentieth birthday," Roth writes as he concludes Marcus's story:

> Marcus Messner, 1932–1952, the only one of his classmates unfortunate enough to be killed in the Korean War, which ended with the signing of an armistice agreement on July 27, 1953, eleven full months after Marcus, had he been able to stomach chapel and keep his mouth shut, would have received his undergraduate degree from Winesburg College—more than likely as class valedictorian—and thus have postponed learning what his uneducated father had been trying so hard to teach him all along: of the terrible, the incomprehensible way one's most banal, incidental, even comical choices achieve the most disproportionate result. (231)

The novel's moral—that our smallest actions can have the most unimaginable consequences—is the bluntest of any that Roth has presented in his fiction, illuminating how history becomes a vindicative and untamable force in Roth's late fiction. It is an argument that the president of Winesburg College articulates at the end of *Indignation*, as he rails against the male undergraduates who have perpetrated a panty raid on the female students. "Beyond your fraternities," President Lentz declares, "history unfolds daily—warfare, bombings, wholesale slaughter, and you are oblivious of it all. Well, you won't be oblivious for long! You can be as stupid as you like, can even give every sign, as you did here on Friday night, of passionately *wanting* to be stupid, but history will catch you in the end. Because history is not the background—history is the stage!" (222).

Despite its emphasis on history, *Indignation*, as Pierpont observes, "appeared to have a grim timeliness when it came out, in the fall of 2008, amid the public outcry over military casualties in Iraq and the government's refusal to allow the publication of photographs of homecoming coffins—both facts mentioned in the review [of the novel] by Charles Simic in *The New York Review of Books.*"[17] While it resonates with the tumultuous state of the US in 2008, *Indignation* also reminds readers of how far removed the past actually is, of how radically American culture has been transformed in the past fifty years. The novel ends with a "Historical Note" that describes how "the social upheavals and transformations and protests of the turbulent decade of the 1960s reached even hidebound, apolitical Winesburg" (232). The panty raid that outrages college administrators in 1951 by 1971 seems almost unthinkably quaint. The sexual agency that Marcus's college girlfriend, Olivia, demonstrates would be seen as commonplace in the coming decades. Marcus simply cannot comprehend it when Olivia performs oral sex on him at the end of one of their dates. "Nor could I believe that what Olivia did she did because she enjoyed doing it," Marcus muses. "The thought was too astonishing even for an open-minded, intelligent boy like me" (58). By defamiliarizing the past, by forcing readers to feel how much has changed in a half century, Roth suggests the story that academic history renders inevitable is anything but.[18]

The significance of history recedes in *The Humbling*, a book that returns to the issues of aging and loss that were central in *Everyman*. The process of becoming "less and less" that Roth alludes to at the end of *Everyman* becomes the central motif that he explores in *The Humbling*. The brief novel revisits the intersection of aging and male sexual desire that Roth explored more fully in *Sabbath's Theater* and *The Dying Animal*. Perhaps not surprisingly, the novel was the least well-received of Roth's later works—in many ways, it interrupted the sustained critical praise that had greeted the bulk of his fiction since *Sabbath's Theater*. In her review for the *New York Times*, Michiko Kakutani described it as "slight, disposable work."[19] Similarly, William Skidelsky argued that *The Humbling* "can hardly be called a novel at all; it is more an old man's sexual fantasy dressed up in the garb of literature."[20] This assessment isn't wholly wrong, yet the novel's lack of grounding would seem to be the point of Roth's thirtieth novel. In many ways, it can be best understood as a meditation on the inexplicable nature of reality. "He lost his magic," Roth writes in the opening sentence, and the book explores what happens when our ability to perform in the world—to both forge a coherent identity and render the chaos of the world into a legible constellation—dissipates.

Whether it is Simon Axler's sudden loss of talent or his much younger girlfriend's mercurial sexual appetite, circumstances within *The Humbling* lack any sort of causality. "Within months of his leaving the hospital," Roth writes early in the novel, "[Simon's] wife's son died of an overdose and the marriage of the occupationless dancer to the occupationless actor ended in divorce, completing yet one more of the many millions of stories of unhappily entwined men and women" (24–5). Such moments are characteristic of Roth's minimal narrative approach in *The Humbling*, and they should be understood as an attempt to prevent fiction from doing what it normally does—package the world in coherent narratives. The stories in *The Humbling* don't make sense—there is no accounting for Simon or Pegeen's behavior, and the story of sexual abuse that a woman confesses to Simon while he is hospitalized for depression in the novel's opening section has no explanation or moral—but that would seem to be the version of lateness that Roth employs in this particular book as he strips fiction of its power. Such a move makes for a less than satisfying book—*The Humbling* offers little of the pleasure that we normally associate with reading fiction—but the absence of that power, the failure of the performance to materialize, is perhaps crucial to the exploration of lateness that Roth pursues in the Nemeses tetralogy.

Roth's final novel, *Nemesis*, moves away from the extreme minimalism that characterizes *The Humbling*. At 280 pages, *Nemesis* is by far the most robust novel of the tetralogy and, in its return to the terrain covered in his earliest fiction, makes for a satisfying conclusion to Roth's fifty-year career. In the novel, Roth returns once more to the Newark of his youth, this time to chronicle a fictional polio outbreak that devastates the city during the summer of 1944. The novel, much like *The Plot Against America*, imagines a crisis that could easily have occurred but, due to the whims of history, never materialized. "Twentieth-century medicine made its phenomenal progress just a little too slowly for us," Arnie Mesnikoff, who serves as the novel's narrator, observes near the conclusion of the book. "Today childhood summers are as sublimely worry-free as they should be. The significance of polio has disappeared completely" (249).

At the center of Roth's final book is a twenty-three-year-old playground director named Bucky Cantor, who is responsible for the well-being of Newark's young as they play countless innings of baseball and jump rope. A "superior athlete and strong" competitor, Bucky nonetheless is declared 4-F due to his poor eyesight and his lack of height, and his guilt over being denied the possibility to participate in the Second World War shapes his reaction to the polio outbreak that summer (11). As he watches the disease spread, Bucky struggles with his guilt while he attempts to determine the best course of action. Persuaded by his girlfriend, Marcia, to escape Newark, Bucky, against his better instincts, abandons his post at the playground and joins her in the Poconos, where she is a counselor at a children's camp called Indian Hill. Once in the Poconos, Bucky soon realizes that he is carrying the disease, that he has been spreading it to the children at the camp, and he may have spread it among those he used to supervise in Newark. Broken by this knowledge, Bucky soon falls ill with polio and subsequently breaks off his relationship with Marcia, choosing to live the rest of his life in relative isolation.

As this summary suggests, *Nemesis* continues the obsession with death and fate that characterizes the tetralogy. Not surprisingly, it also extends the explicit narrative difficulty that is evident in *Indignation* and *The Humbling*, when Roth unexpectedly reveals that Bucky Cantor's story is not being told from the perspective of an anonymous heterodiegetic narrator, but instead by Arnie Mesnikoff, who was one of the boys stricken with polio at the playground that summer. This revelation, which occurs on page 108 of the novel and for which there has been little, if any, textual preparation—the only clue might be the narrator's proclivity to refer to Bucky as Mr. Cantor, suggesting that Arnie still sees Bucky as the powerful hero from his childhood—forces readers to alter, rather radically, their understanding of the narrative. The narrative immediately dissolves from being a definitive account of Bucky Cantor's experience to a retelling of that history from a particular perspective.

What makes *Nemesis* a particularly satisfying conclusion to this series is Roth's return to the narrative strategy that he employed to such great success in the American Trilogy, as he once again uses one character as the medium through which we are told another character's story. In particular, *Nemesis* recalls the character dynamics that Roth established in *American Pastoral,* as a now older man attempts to imagine the inner life of a boyhood idol (and Bucky, with all of his bland goodness, seems to be a simplified version of the Swede). This nod to *American Pastoral* seems purposeful, especially considering the way *The Humbling* recalls the sexual furor and suicidal depression of *Sabbath's Theater.*

Roth reveals little about Arnie until the novel's final section, in which Arnie describes how he was reunited with Bucky during the spring of 1971 after a happenstance meeting at a busy Newark intersection. Even in this section Roth reveals very little about his narrator; Arnie describes his successful career as a mechanical engineer designing home modifications to better serve those who require a wheelchair (241–2). There are moments of lyrical grace to Arnie's narration: not surprisingly, he slows things down when he is describing playing baseball all summer long and when he is imagining Marcia's youthful body, describing her body as "small and slim, with beautifully formed, lightly muscled legs and thin arms and fragile wrists and tiny breasts, affixed high on her chest, and nipples that were soft, pale, and unprotuberant" (166). There is also a particularly evocative passage where Arnie describes Bucky enjoying a peach on Dr. Steinberg's porch and asking the physician's permission to marry his daughter. The narrator takes a pointed pleasure in describing Bucky: "wholly unprepared for the moment but unable to contain himself, he placed the pit into an ashtray, leaned forward, and compress[ed] his sticky hands tightly together between his knees" (107). Such moments of pleasure are rare in Roth's final novels, and these bursts of lyricism distinguish *Nemesis* from the other volumes in the tetralogy. Nevertheless, Roth seems less interested in exploring Arnie's motivations as a narrator—as was the case with Zuckerman throughout the American Trilogy—and the emphasis seems to be on the story itself. There is an old-fashioned quality to Roth's approach in *Nemesis* as he allows the story to speak for itself.

For in the end, Arnie seems to possess little interest in interpreting Bucky's life story beyond the most basic moral that Roth has been insisting upon throughout the tetralogy: that of chance's power to devastate an individual's (or community's) existence. "Sometimes you're lucky and sometimes you're not," Arnie muses towards the novel's conclusion. "Any biography is chance, and, beginning at conception, chance—the tyranny of contingency—is everything. Chance is what I believed Mr. Cantor meant when he was decrying what he called God" (242–3). The moral of Bucky's story, from Arnie's perspective, is that Bucky mistakenly ascribes meaning to the meaningless. It is a moral that Arnie makes explicit near the end of the novel: "Bucky's conception of God, as I thought I understood it, was of omnipotent being whose nature and purpose was to be adduced not from his biblical evidence but from his irrefutable historical proof, gleaned during a lifetime passed on this planet in the middle of the twentieth century. His conception of God was of an omnipotent being who was a union not of three persons in one Godhead, as in Christianity, but of two—a sick fuck and an evil genius" (264–5). This passage wonderfully underscores the message that has pervaded Roth's fiction since *The Plot Against America*, of how history itself gives artificial shape and meaning to the chaos that defines our experience. "Turned wrong way round, the relentless unforeseen was what we schoolchildren studied as 'History,' harmless history, where everything unexpected in its own time is chronicled on the page as inevitable," the narrator Philip Roth observes in *The Plot Against America*. "The terror of the unforeseen is what the science of history hides, turning a disaster into an epic" (113–4). Arnie's response to this problem—how do we account for the seemingly meaningless horrors of the twentieth century?—is to accept them: he refuses to accord significance to what happened to him and simply moves on to have a career and a family. He refuses to ask the questions that drive Bucky into isolation.

However, it is in the asking questions that Roth's fiction has garnered its power, and Arnie's refusal to ask these questions makes *Nemesis* a troubling novel. That Roth concludes his career in the Nemeses tetralogy by refusing to ask these questions is perhaps the most disconcerting aspect of Roth's late fiction. That said, his insistence on what fiction can capture—how it can animate the "relentless unforeseen," how it can depict the circumstances that alter our personal and national fortunes—is the great accomplishment of *The Plot Against America* and the Nemeses tetralogy, his late work insisting on the necessity of storytelling as our only, albeit flawed, way of understanding the world in which we find ourselves. From *Goodbye, Columbus* to *Nemesis*, Roth maintained his belief in fiction's capacity for helping us better understand ourselves and our nation; his thirty-one novels offer a complex and challenging portrait of a half-century of American life.

NOTES

Chapter 1—Understanding Philip Roth

    1. Remnick, "Philip Roth's Propulsive Force."

    2. Wood, "The Unceasing Necessity of Philip Roth."

    3. Said, *On Late Style*, 17.

    4. Leith, "Philip Roth Attacks 'Orgy of Narcissism' post-Sept. 11."

    5. To clarify, the letter would seem to be a product of Zuckerman's imagination; he is ventriloquizing the position he imagines Maria might take.

    6. Robert Milder offers an especially compelling reading of how Roth depicts the violence of the 1960s in *American Pastoral*. Comparing *American Pastoral* with Virginia Woolf's *To the Lighthouse* (1927), Milder observes that both Roth and Woolf conceptualize the historical traumas, the violence of the 1960s and World War I, that shaped their adult lives: "Who or what is responsible for the danger lurking in life—history? The perverse human impulse toward destruction? A principle of entropy in the universe? Godlessness? Bad luck? Neither Roth nor Woolf knows the source of the unexpected and horrific, only the recurring fact of it." See Milder, "Transactions with Disorder," 161.

    7. In recounting Roth's biography and family history, I've consulted the chronology included in *Why Write?: Collected Nonfiction 1960–2013*, the ninth and final volume in The Library of America's collection of Roth's work. See *Why Write?*, 407–18. Claudia Roth Pierpont's *Roth Unbound*, Blake Bailey's *Philip Roth: The Biography*, and Ira Nadel's *Philip Roth: A Counterlife* have all been useful in establishing details of Roth's biography. A useful chronology of Roth's education, Army experience, and early career can also be found in *The Cambridge Companion to Philip Roth*, edited by Timothy Parrish, ix–xi. The biography included in *Critical Insights: Philip Roth* also provides a comprehensive overview of Roth's early years. *See Critical Insights: Philip Roth*, edited by Aimee Pozorski, 239–42.

    8. Nadel describes how "Roth began what would be a lifetime as a reader after his brother, one summer, brought home the student newspaper from Pratt Institute of Art in Brooklyn, where he had been studying. It included a list of recommended summer reading," which included Thomas Wolfe's *Look Homeward Angel*, Sinclair Lewis's *Babbitt*, and Sherwood Anderson's *Winsesburg, Ohio*, that jumpstarted Roth's interest in literature. See Nadel, *Philip Roth: A Counterlife*, 46. Bailey details the ways in which the young Roth idealized his older brother. See Bailey, *Philip Roth*, 34–6.

    9. Portions of the rest of this chapter appeared in a different form in "Life." See Shipe, "Life," 11–16.

10. Bailey, *Philip Roth*, 22–3. For more on Roth's childhood relationship with his parents see Bailey, 22–36.

11. Ibid., 21.

12. Pierpont, *Roth Unbound*, 17.

13. Remnick, "Into the Clear." Debra Shostak also highlights this quotation in the introduction to her *Philip Roth—Countertexts, Counterlives,* and I was reminded of it when rereading her excellent book. See Shostak, 10.

14. Perlstein, *Nixonland*, 190.

15. Bailey details how Roth as a high school senior considered attending the University of Missouri to study journalism, but the family's limited financial resources and his father's opposition prevented him from applying. "Roth had hoped to get at least as far afield as Rutgers' main campus in New Brunswick, but he was turned down for scholarships both there and at the local campus in downtown Newark, almost certainly because he had to report his father's income—a decent figure now that Herman was district manager—but couldn't mention the man's even more impressive debts, lest the information get back to Metropolitan Life." See Bailey, *Philip Roth*, 68.

16. Nadel, *Philip Roth: A Counterlife*, 81.

17. Roth, "In Prague."

18. Nadel, *Philip Roth: A Counterlife*, 268.

19. Taylor, *Here We Are*, 159.

20. Bloom, "His Long Ordeal by Laughter."

21. Posnock, *Philip Roth's Rude Truth*, 50.

22. McGrath, "No Longer Writer Philip Roth Has Plenty to Say."

23. Pierpont, *Roth Unbound*, 160. Pierpont discusses Roth's medical emergencies of the late 1980s on pages 159–60.

24. McGrath, "Zuckerman's Alter Brain."

25. While Zuckerman makes his debut in *My Life as a Man*, he is better known as the central protagonist of *The Ghost Writer, Zuckerman Unbound, The Anatomy Lesson, The Prague Orgy, The Counterlife,* and *Exit Ghost* as well as the narrative voice behind the American Trilogy.

26. Royal, *Philip Roth: New Perspectives on an American Author*, 187.

27. Remnick, "Philip Roth Says Enough." In his article, Remnick quotes extensively from the original French interview, which can be found at: https://www.lesinrocks.com /2012/10/07/livres/livres/philip-roth-nemesis-sera-mon-dernier-livre/

28. Schuessler, "Philip Roth Says He Has Given His Last Public Reading."

29. In addition to collecting material for Bailey, Roth also composed two unpublished documents: "Notes for My Biographer," a long rebuke of Claire Bloom's depiction of their marriage in *Leaving a Doll's House,* and "Notes on a Slander-Monger," a response to Ross Miller's aborted biography of Roth (Miller had been Roth's first choice to write his biography). Neither document has been published, but Bailey incorporates information from them in *Philip Roth: The Biography.*

30. The information on Bailey and the fate of *Philip Roth: The Biography* is current as of September 2021.

31. For a more detailed account of how the Bailey scandal impacted Roth's legacy, see Alter, Alexandra, and Jennifer Schuessler, "What Happens to Philip Roth's Legacy Now?" For an insightful reading of Roth's treatment of women in his fiction, see David Gooblar's "Introduction: Roth and Women." Gooblar's essay offers a useful framework for reconsidering Roth's female characters. Also helpful on this question is Miriam

Jaffe-Foger and Aimee Pozorski's essay on the Nemeses tetralogy in which they discover a "maturity" in Roth's depiction of his female characters in his final novels. See Jaffe-Foger and Pozorski, "'Anything but fragile and yielding'," 93.

32. Rushdie, "How Philip Roth Became a Political Prophet."

33. McGrath, "No Longer Writing, Philip Roth Still Has Plenty to Say."

Chapter 2—Early Works

1. Pierpont, *Roth Unbound*, 13.

2. Aarons, "American Jewish Identity in Roth's Short Fiction," 11.

3. Gooblar, *The Major Phases of Philip Roth*, 14.

4. Avishai, *Promiscuous*, 3.

5. Gooblar, *The Major Phases of Philip Roth*, 45.

6. Trilling, "The Uncomplaining Homosexuals."

7. Howe, "Philip Roth Reconsidered."

8. Samuel Cohen similarly critiques Trilling and Howe's reviews for not seeing "the note of ambiguity in Roth's presentation of Alex's attempts to free himself." Cohen, *After the End of History*, 79.

9. In his discussion of Roth's relationship to the late 1960s, Cohen also cites this passage as evidence that Roth did not see *Portnoy's Complaint* as an act of personal liberation but instead an artistic one, the voice and form of the novel freeing Roth from his indebtedness to his literary predecessors. See Cohen, *After the End of History*, 78–9.

10. Avishai, *Promiscuous*, 165.

11. *The Breast*, which is the first of the Kepesh books, will be discussed in chapter four.

12. Shostak, *Philip Roth—Countertexts, Counterlives*, 79.

13. Roth, "On The Air."

14. McDonald, "Our Gang."

15. Shostak, *Philip Roth—Countertexts, Counterlives*, 171.

Chapter 3—The Writing Life

1. At the beginning of his final novel, *Nemesis*, Roth lists the "Zuckerman Books" as: *The Ghost Writer, Zuckerman Unbound, The Anatomy Lesson, The Prague Orgy, The Counterlife, American Pastoral, I Married a Communist, The Human Stain,* and *Exit Ghost*. Roth interestingly excludes *My Life as a Man*, which is the novel in which Zuckerman is introduced, from the list, placing that novel in "Other Books" section, a move that relegates that novel, perhaps unfairly, to the sidelines of Roth's oeuvre.

2. Pierpont, *Roth Unbound*, 113.

3. In her monograph on the Zuckerman series, Pia Masiero rightly emphasizes the inconsistency that defines Roth's characterization of Zuckerman, arguing that "Nathan Zuckerman is crucially reshaped and acquires new narrative functions" throughout Roth's work. See Masiero, *Philip Roth and the Zuckerman Books*, 9.

4. McGrath, "Zuckerman's Alter Brain."

5. Lonoff would seem to be partially modeled on Bernard Malamud, who taught at Bennington College in Vermont and who lived in "remote clapboard farmhouse." According to Bailey, Roth had visited Malamud in the late 1960s and had seen "a mysterious young woman sitting on the floor sorting manuscripts—an impression he saved for *The Ghost Writer*, along with aspects of Malamud's conversation." Unbeknownst to Roth, Malamud had carried on an affair with a student in the early 1960s, a relationship

that uncannily resembles Lonoff's affair with Amy Bellette in the novel. Bailey also notes how aspects of Lonoff's character and backstory came from Roth's friendship with the painter Philip Guston and the literary critic Philip Rahv. See Bailey, *Philip Roth*, 321; 328–30.

6. Pierpont cites "Epstein" and "Defender of the Faith" as the stories that "Higher Education" most closely resembles. See Pierpont, *Roth Unbound*, 110.

7. Hayes offers an especially insightful reading of Roth's use of the James story, connecting it with the novel's larger desire to respond to the "French-lit priests" (Foucault, Barthes) who came into critical vogue during the late 1970s. See Hayes, *Philip Roth: Fiction and Power*, 160–61.

8. Gooblar, *The Major Phases of Philip Roth*, 80.

9. Ibid., 82.

10. Ibid., 84.

11. Charles McGrath, in his essay, "Roth/Updike," cites this moment in his consideration of Roth and Updike's relationship.

12. Kartiganer, "*Zuckerman Bound*: The Celebrant of Silence," 40.

13. Jacques Berlinerblau offers a thoughtful reading of Roth's sometimes myopic views of post-1967 Newark. See Berlinerblau, *The Philip Roth We Don't Know: Sex, Race and Autobiography*, 21–36.

14. Felt would seem to be modeled on the Alan Lelchuk, whose debut novel, *American Mischief* (1973), Roth championed and with whom he maintained a friendship for much of the 1970s. In *The Anatomy Lesson*, Felt receives a request from the critic Milton Appel to approach Zuckerman to write a letter in support of Israel in the wake of the Yom Kippur War (1973), which mirrors how Irving Howe wrote to Lelchuk in 1973 about the possibility of approaching Roth to write such a letter to the *New York Times*. Lelchuk would also seem to the model for the sexually adventurous poet Ralph Baumgarten in *The Professor of Desire*. See Bailey, *Philip Roth*, 372–77; 678–79. Thanks to Louis Gordon for proving more information on Roth and Lelchuck's relationship and for pointing out that Roth named the Felt character after one of the primary suspects for Deep Throat's actual identity.

15. Howe, "Philip Roth Reconsidered."

16. Nadel, *Philip Roth: A Counterlife*, 282.

17. Wood, "My Hero: Philip Roth."

18. Pierpont, *Roth Unbound*, 145.

19. Rothstein, "Philip Roth and the World of 'What If?'," 199.

20. Shostak, *Philip Roth—Countertexts, Counterlives*, 131–2.

21. Said, *On Late Style*, 17. I discuss the political implications of Roth's late style more fully in my essay "*Exit Ghost* and the Politics of Late Style."

Chapter 4—Sex and the Serious Life

1. Shostak, "Roth and Gender," 112.

2. In "Roth and Gender," Shostak makes a similar argument, asserting that "Roth's work can appear as much a prescient critique of misogynist attitudes as a purveyor of them. Even in first person narratives, Roth gives us the opportunity to gain distance on the objectifying male, to register our own ambivalence alongside the character's." Shostak, "Roth and Gender," 112–3.

3. McGrath, "No Longer Writing, Philip Roth Still Has Plenty to Say."

4. Witcombe, "In the Roth Archives," 45.

5. McCrum, "A Conversation with Philip Roth."

6. I discuss the connection between *The Breast* and celebrity in the chapter "Twilight of the Superheroes: Philip Roth, Celebrity and the End of Print Culture." See Shipe, *Roth and Celebrity*, 101–18.

7. Witcombe, "In the Roth Archives," 53. Witcombe's essay offers a highly thoughtful reading of how Roth revised the text of *The Breast* when the novel was republished in 1980 and then again in 1989: "Roth's changes to the 1980 version attempt a fusion between frustration and coherence, adding rhetorical questions and quotation marks—editing the section to make the text more articulate and its narrator less frantic" (53).

8. Pierpont, *Roth Unbound*, 107.

9. Shechner, *Up Society's Ass, Copper!*, 64

10. Shostak, *Philip Roth—Countertexts, Counterlives*, 60.

11. Ibid., 64.

Chapter 5—Personality Crisis

1. Pierpont, *Roth Unbound*, 159.

2. For more information on Roth's health crises at the time, see Roth Pierpont, *Roth Unbound*, 159–60; Nadel, *Philip Roth: A Counterlife*, 330–31; Bailey, *Philip Roth*, 488–89, 516–19.

3. Nadel, *Philip Roth: A Counterlife*, 331.

4. In the official "Books by Philip Roth" page included in his final novel, *Nemesis*, Roth groups these four books, alongside *The Plot Against America* (2004), as the "Roth Books." While Roth's decision to feature himself as the protagonist of *The Plot Against America* certainly connects it to these earlier works, the historical and political questions that drive that later novel are much different than the more personal questions Roth pursues throughout the earlier four books.

5. Bailey reports that Roth in the early 1990s considered publishing the four books as a single volume entitled "AGAINST ITSELF/The Autobiography of an Antithesis," which would be his final book and would offer "a multivalent self-portrait." Bailey, *Philip Roth*, 544.

6. Shechner, *Up Society's Ass, Copper*, 127.

7. Updike, "Recruiting Raw Nerves," 298.

8. For more information on Demjanjuk's history see, Douglas, *The Right Wrong Man*, 1–16.

Chapter 6—Back in the USA

1. McGrath, "Zuckerman's Alter Brain."

2. While *Operation Shylock* won the PEN/Faulkner award, Roth remained disappointed by the mixed reviews the novel received. Claudia Roth Pierpont reports how Roth was stung by John Updike's somewhat ambivalent review of *Operation Shylock* in the *New Yorker*. "[The review] had to hurt," Pierpont writes. "Whatever Roth thought about the capacities of professional reviewers, he had an unflagging respect for Updike's opinion." Pierpont, *Roth Unbound*, 184.

3. Of the American Trilogy, only *I Married a Communist*, the second installment in the series, did not collect any major literary awards.

4. Marcus, *The Shape of Things to Come*, 43.

5. Scott, "In Search of the Best."

6. Gooblar, *The Major Phases of Philip Roth*, 132.

7. Ibid., 132.

8. Shostak, "Introduction: Roth's America," 12.

9. Hutcheon, *A Poetics of Postmodernism*, 5.

10. Taylor, *Here We Are*, 111.

11. Hayes, *Philip Roth: Fiction and Power*, 113.

12. Pierpont, *Roth Unbound*, 207.

13. Knowles, "'How the Other Half Lives': *American Pastoral* and Roth's Other Europe."

14. McGrath, "Roth's Alter Brain."

15. Pia Masiero offers a perceptive reading of how Zuckerman reimagines the Swede's life. See Masiero, *Philip Roth and the Zuckerman Books*, 139–61.

16. In his review of the novel, Todd Gitlin observes that "Roth's sixties are chronologically odd. Merry bombs the store on February 3, 1968—before the Columbia occupation, before the Chicago Götterdämmerung and during the Tet offensive, when the antiwar movement was only just turning (in a phrase of that time) 'from protest to resistance.' The militant vanguard wasn't anywhere near bombing. Two years would pass before the Weather Underground's 11th Street townhouse in New York City blew up, killing three of their own." See Gitlin, "Weather Girl."

17. Didion, "Slouching Towards Bethlehem," 123.

18. Milder, "Transactions with Disorder," 151.

19. Bailey reports that the kiss was based on an encounter with Roth's stepdaughter, Holly (whom Bailey gives the pseudonym Helen), who was the daughter of Roth's first wife, Maggie, from her first marriage and with whom Roth developed a close relationship: "Unlike Swede Levov in *American Pastoral*, Roth did not oblige [the request to be kissed], and he would have been wise, too, not to mention the episode to his wife." See Bailey, *Philip Roth*, 216. Nadel also comments on how Holly served as a potential model for Merry Levov, noting that Roth referred to her as "Hanoi Helen" in *The Facts*. Nadel also usefully charts out how incest and sexual trauma are reoccurring themes in Roth's fiction, appearing in *When She Was Good, Portnoy's Complaint, My Life as a Man, American Pastoral, The Human Stain, Exit Ghost*, and *The Humbling*. See Nadel, *Philip Roth: A Counterlife*, 233–35.

20. Goldberg, "'Incest, Blood, and Shame. Are They Not Enough to Make One Feel Sinful?': Miltonic Figurations of Incest and Disobedience in Philip Roth's *American Pastoral*," *Philip Roth Studies* 16.1 (2020): 38.

21. Cohen, *After the End of History*, 87.

22. Podhoretz, "The Adventures of Philip Roth." For additional conservative readings of the novel see Gordon, "The Critique of the Pastoral, Utopia, and the American Dream in *American Pastoral*" and Schechner, *Up Society's Ass, Copper!*, 154–73.

23. See Ira Nadel's "*I Married a Communist*: The Book! The Movie! The Commie Threat!" for a more detailed history of *The Woman on Pier 13* and how Roth's novel engages with Hughes's film.

24. Taylor, *Here We Are*, 159.

25. Pierpont, *Roth Unbound*, 236.

26. Ibid., 241.

27. Posnock, *Philip Roth's Rude Truth*, 195.

28. Pozorski, *Roth and Trauma*, 81.

Chapter 7—Late Works

1. I would also add the final Kepesh volume (*The Dying Animal*) and the final Zuckerman novel (*Exit Ghost*) to this grouping of Roth's late work, as both novels are thematically and stylistically similar to the slim novels that constitute the Nemeses tetralogy.

2. The essay, included in *Why Write?: Collected Nonfiction 1960–2013*, was originally published the *New York Times Book Review* on September 19, 2004 under the title "The Story Behind 'The Plot Against America'."

3. Kimmage, *In History's Grip*, 6.

4. In his review of the novel, Jonathan Yardley argues that *The Plot Against America* can be read as Roth's critical response to the Bush administration: "Now, with the United States at unceasing risk of terrorist attack and with many Americans fearful that civil liberties are being compromised as the government attempts to fight terrorism, Roth gives new currency to the old phrase—indeed, deliberately employs it *as The Plot Against America* approaches its climax. "It can't happen here?" a prominent American politician asks a large audience in New York City in October 1942. "My friends, it is happening here. . . ." See Yardley, "Homeland Insecurity."

5. Taylor, *Here We Are*, 120.

6. Connolly, *Philip Roth and the American Liberal Tradition*, 235.

7. Pierpont, *Roth Unbound*, 273.

8. Daniel Grausam offers a particular incisive reading of the lack of the butterfly effect in the novel, and he also highlights Roth's mention of Robert Kennedy's murder. See Grausam, "After The Post(al)."

9. Parrish, "Autobiography and History in Roth's *The Plot Against America*, or What Happened When Hitler Came to New Jersey," 146.

10. Coetzee, "On the Moral Brink."

11. Adorno, "Late Style in Beethoven," 566.

12. Said, *On Late Style*, 24.

13. Taylor, *Here We Are*, 123.

14. Roth makes this position very clear in a 2006 interview with the German news magazine *Der Spiegel*. See Volker Hage, "Old Age is a Massacre. *Spiegel* Interview with Philip Roth," *Der Spiegel*, August 25, 2006. https://www.spiegel.de/international/spiegel-interview-with-philip-roth-old-age-is-a-massacre-a-433607.html.

15. Nadel, *Philip Roth: A Counterlife*, 12–13; 81–82.

16. In the "Joe College" chapter of *The Facts*, Roth describes why he left Newark Rutgers after his freshman year and transferred to Bucknell University: "In all, it was an unoutlandish little college town of the kind I'd seen before only in movies with Kay Kyser or June Allyson, not so much subdued or genteel, and certainly not posh or gentrified, but instead suited for the coziest, most commonplace dreams of order" (46). In *Indignation*, Marcus offers a similar explanation for transferring to the bucolic Winesburg College, which Roth sets in rural Ohio, describing the campus as looking like "the backdrop for one of those Technicolor college movie musicals" (18). Similarly, Marcus transfers from Newark to escape the tirades of his overprotective father, a situation similar to the one Roth describes with his own father in the "Joe College" chapter.

Claudia Roth Pierpont also usefully suggests the ways *Indignation* reimagines Roth's time at Bucknell. See Pierpont, *Roth Unbound*, 299.

17. Pierpont, *Roth Unbound*, 300.

18. This argument is developed more fully in my earlier essay on *Indignation*. See Shipe, "After the Fall: The Terror of History in Philip Roth's *Indignation*."

19. Kakutani, "Two Storytellers, Singing the Blues."

20. Skidelsky, "*The Humbling* by Philip Roth."

BIBLIOGRAPHY

Works by Philip Roth

BOOKS (LISTED CHRONOLOGICALLY)

Goodbye, Columbus and Five Short Stories. Boston: Houghton Mifflin, 1959.

Letting Go. New York: Random House, 1962.

When She Was Good. New York: Random House, 1967.

Portnoy's Complaint. New York: Random House, 1969.

Our Gang. New York: Random House, 1971.

The Breast. New York: Holt, Rinehart and Winston, 1972.

The Great American Novel. New York: Holt, Rinehart and Winston, 1973.

My Life as a Man. New York: Holt, Rinehart and Winston, 1974.

Reading Myself and Others. New York: Farrar, Straus and Giroux, 1975.

The Professor of Desire. New York: Farrar, Straus and Giroux, 1977.

The Ghost Writer. New York: Farrar, Straus and Giroux, 1979.

Zuckerman Unbound. New York: Farrar, Straus and Giroux, 1981.

The Anatomy Lesson. New York: Farrar, Straus and Giroux, 1983.

The Prague Orgy. New York: Farrar, Straus and Giroux, 1985. Originally published as the epilogue to *Zuckerman Bound*, a volume that included *The Ghost Writer*, *Zuckerman Unbound*, and *The Anatomy Lesson*. Farrar, Straus and Giroux, 699–784.

The Counterlife. Farrar, Straus and Giroux, 1986.

The Facts: A Novelist's Autobiography. Farrar, Straus and Giroux, 1988.

Deception: A Novel. New York: Simon and Schuster, 1990.

Patrimony: A True Story. New York: Simon and Schuster, 1991.

Operation Shylock: A Confession. New York: Simon and Schuster, 1993.

Sabbath's Theater. Boston: Houghton Mifflin, 1995.

American Pastoral: Boston: Houghton Mifflin, 1997.

I Married a Communist. Boston: Houghton Mifflin, 1998.

The Human Stain. Boston: Houghton Mifflin, 2000.

The Dying Animal. Boston: Houghton Mifflin, 2001.

Shop Talk: A Writer and His Colleagues and Their Work. Boston: Houghton Mifflin, 2001.

The Plot Against America. Boston: Houghton Mifflin, 2004.

Everyman. Boston: Houghton Mifflin, 2006.

Exit Ghost. Boston: Houghton Mifflin, 2007.

Indignation. Boston: Houghton Mifflin, 2008.

The Humbling. Boston: Houghton Mifflin, 2009.

Nemesis. Boston: Houghton Mifflin, 2010.

Why Write? Collected Nonfiction 1960–2013. New York: Library of America, 2017.

UNCOLLECTED WORK

"In Prague," *New Yorker*, May 3, 2013. https://www.newyorker.com/books/page-turner
    /in-prague.

"On The Air," *New American Review* 10 (1970): 7–49.

Secondary Sources

Aarons, Victoria. "American Jewish Identity in Roth's Short Fiction." In *The Cambridge
    Companion to Philip Roth*, edited by Timothy Parrish, 9–21. Cambridge: Cambridge
    University Press, 2007.

Adorno, Theodor. "Late Style in Beethoven." In *Essays on Music*, edited by Richard
    Lepper, 564–8. Berkeley: University of California Press, 2002.

Alter, Alexandra, and Jennifer Schuessler, "What Happens to Philip Roth's Legacy Now?"
    New York Times, June 4, 2021, https://www.nytimes.com/2021/06/04/books/philip-
    roth-biography-blake-bailey.html.

Avishai, Bernard. *Promiscuous: Portnoy's Complaint and Our Doomed Pursuit of Hap-
    piness.* New Haven, CT: Yale University Press, 2012.

Bailey, Blake. *Philip Roth: The Biography.* New York: W.W. Norton & Company, 2021.

Berlinerblau, Jacques. *The Philip Roth We Don't Know: Sex, Race, and Autobiography.*
    Charlottesville: University of Virginia Press, 2021.

Bloom, Claire. *Leaving a Doll's House.* New York, Little, Brown, 1996.

Bloom, Harold. "His Long Ordeal by Laughter." Review of *Zuckerman Bound*, by Philip
    Roth. *New York Times Book Review*, May 19, 1985, http://movies2.nytimes.com/books
    /98/10/11/specials/roth-unbound.html.

Brauner, David. *Philip Roth.* Manchester: Manchester University Press, 2007.

———. "'What was not supposed to happen had happened and was supposed to hap-
    pen had not happened': Subverting History in *American Pastoral*." In *Philip Roth:
    American Pastoral, The Human Stain, The Plot Against America*, ed. Debra Shostak,
    19–32. New York: Continuum Books, 2011.

Baumgarten, Murray and Barbara Gottfried. *Understanding Philip Roth.* Columbia:
    University of South Carolina Press, 1990.

Cheyette, Brian. *Diasporas of the Mind: Jewish and Postcolonial Writing and the Night-
    mare of History.* New Haven, CT: Yale University Press, 2014.

Cohen, Samuel. *After the End of History: American Fiction in the 1990s.* Iowa City:
    University of Iowa Press, 2009.

Connolly, Andy. *Philip Roth and the American Liberal Tradition.* Lanham: Lexington
    Books, 2017.

Coetzee, J. M. "On the Moral Brink." Review of *Nemesis*, by Philip Roth. *The New York
    Review of Books*, October 28, 2010, https://www.nybooks.com/articles/2010/10/28
    /moral-brink/.

Dickstein, Morris. *Leopards in the Temple: The Transformation of American Fiction
    1945–1970.* Cambridge, MA: Harvard University Press, 2002.

Didion, Joan. "Slouching Towards Bethlehem." In *Slouching Towards Bethlehem*,
    84–127. New York: Farrar, Straus and Giroux, 1968.

Douglas, Lawrence. *The Right Wrong Man: John Demjanjuk and the Last Great Nazi War Crimes Trial*. Princeton: Princeton University Press, 2016.

Finkielkraut, Alan. "The Ghosts of Roth." In *Conversations with Philip Roth*, edited by George Searles, 120–30. Jackson: University of Mississippi Press, 1992.

Gitlin, Todd. "Weather Girl." Review of *American Pastoral*, by Philip Roth. *The Nation*, May 12, 1997.

Goldberg, RL. "'Incest, Blood, and Shame. Are They Not Enough to Make One Feel Sinful?': Miltonic Figurations of Incest and Disobedience in Philip Roth's *American Pastoral*." *Philip Roth Studies* 16.1 (2020): 33–52.

Gooblar, David. "Introduction: Roth and Women." *Philip Roth Studies*. 8.1 (Spring 2012): 7–15.

———. *The Major Phases of Philip Roth*. London: Continuum Books, 2011.

Gordon, Andrew. "The Critique of the Pastoral, Utopia, and the American Dream in *American Pastoral*." In *Philip Roth: American Pastoral, The Human Stain, The Plot Against America*, edited by Debra Shostak, 33–43. New York: Continuum Books, 2011.

Gornick, Vivian. "Saul Bellow, Philip Roth, and the End of the Jew as Metaphor." In *The Men in My Life*, 85–130. Cambridge, MA: The MIT Press, 2008.

Grant, Linda. "The Wrath of Roth." Review of *I Married a Communist*, by Philip Roth. *The Guardian*, Oct 3, 1998, https://www.theguardian.com/books/1998/oct/03/fiction.philiproth.

Grausam, Daniel. "After The Post(al)" *American Literary History* 23.3 (2011): 625–642.

Hage, Volker. "Old Age is a Massacre. *Spiegel* Interview with Philip Roth." *Der Spiegel*, August 25, 2006, https://www.spiegel.de/international/spiegel-interview-with-philip-roth-old-age-is-a-massacre-a-433607.html.

Halio, Jay. *Philip Roth Revisited*. New York: Twayne Publishers, 1992.

Hayes, Patrick. *Philip Roth: Fiction and Power*. Oxford: Oxford University Press, 2014.

Howe, Irving. "Philip Roth Reconsidered." *Commentary*, December 1972, https://www.commentarymagazine.com/articles/irving-howe/philip-roth-reconsidered/

Hutcheon, Linda. *A Poetics of Postmodernism: History, Theory, Fiction*. New York: Routledge, 1988.

Ivanova, Velichka. "My Own Foe from the Other Gender: (Mis)representing Women in *The Dying Animal*. *Philip Roth Studies*. 8.1 (Spring 2012): 31–44.

Jaffe-Foger, Miriam and Aimee Pozorski. "'Anything but fragile and yielding': Women in Roth's Recent Tetralogy." *Philip Roth Studies*. 8.1 (Spring 2012): 81–94.

Kakutani, Michiko. "Two Storytellers, Singing the Blues." Review of *The Humbling*, by Philip Roth and *Nocturnes,* by Kazuo Ishiguro. *New York Times*, October 22, 2009, https://www.nytimes.com/2009/10/23/books/23book.html.

Kaprièlian, Nelly. "Philip Roth: 'Némésis sera mon dernier livre'." *Les Inrockuptibles,* October 7, 2012, https://www.lesinrocks.com/livres/philip-roth-nemesis-sera-mon-dernier-livre-144702-07-10-2012/.

Kartiganer, Donald M. "*Zuckerman Bound*: The Celebrant of Silence." In *The Cambridge Companion to Philip Roth*, edited by Timothy Parrish, 35–51. Cambridge: Cambridge University Press, 2007.

Keller, Julia. "Philip Roth Hates Women." *The Chicago Tribune*, June 1, 2006, https://www.chicagotribune.com/news/ct-xpm-2006-06-01-0605310232-story.html.

Kimmage, Michael. *In History's Grip: Philip Roth's Newark Trilogy*. Stanford: Stanford University Press, 2012.

Knowles, Jack. "'How the Other Half Lives': *American Pastoral* and Roth's Other Europe." *Philip Roth Studies* 16.1 (2020): 14–32.

Leith, Sam. "Philip Roth Attacks 'Orgy of Narcissism' post-Sept. 11." *Daily Telegraph*, October 5, 2002, https://www.telegraph.co.uk/education/4792421/Philip-Roth-attacks -orgy-of-narcissism-post-Sept-11.html.

Marcus, Greil. *The Shape of Things to Come: Prophecy and the American Voice*. New York: Farrar, Straus and Giroux, 2006.

Masiero, Pia. *Philip Roth and the Zuckerman Books: The Making of a Storyworld*. Amherst: Cambria Press, 2011.

McCrum, Robert. "A Conversation with Philip Roth." *The Observer*, July 1, 2001, https://www.theguardian.com/books/2001/jul/01/fiction.philiproth1.

McDonald, Dwight. "Our Gang." Review of *Our Gang*, by Philip Roth. *New York Times*, November 7, 1971, https://archive.nytimes.com/www.nytimes.com/books/98 /10/11/specials/roth-gang.html

McGrath, Charles. "Goodbye, Frustration: Pen Put Aside, Roth Talks." *New York Times*, November 17, 2012, https://www.nytimes.com/2012/11/18/books/struggle-over -philip-roth-reflects-on-putting-down-his-pen.html.

———. "No Longer Writing, Philip Roth Still Has Plenty to Say." *New York Times*, January 16, 2018, https://www.nytimes.com/2018/01/16/books/review/philip-roth -interview.html.

———. "Roth/Updike." *The Hudson Review*, Autumn 2019, https://hudsonreview .com/2019/10/roth-updike/#.YJoOnZNKhJU.

———. "Zuckerman's Alter Brain." *New York Times Book Review*, May 7, 2000, http://movies2.nytimes.com/books/00/05/07/reviews/000507.07mcgrat.html.

Milder, Robert. "Transactions with Disorder: *American Pastoral* and *To the Lighthouse*." *Studies in the Novel* 53.2 (2021): 141–64.

Nadel, Ira. "*I Married a Communist:* The Book! The Movie! The Commie Threat!" *Philip Roth Studies* 16.2 (2020): 3–15.

———. *Philip Roth: A Counterlife*. Oxford: Oxford University Press, 2021.

O'Donoghue, Gerard. "Roth on the American Screen: 'Serious' Literature and Popular Democracy." *Philip Roth Studies* 16.1 (2020): 53–73.

Parrish, Timothy, "Autobiography and History in Roth's *Plot Against America*, or What Happened When Hitler Came to New Jersey." In *Philip Roth: American Pastoral, The Human Stain, The Plot Against America*, ed. Debra Shostak, 145–60. New York: Continuum Books, 2011.

———. ed. *The Cambridge Companion to Philip Roth*. Cambridge: Cambridge University Press, 2007.

Perlstein, Rick. *Nixonland: The Rise of a President and the Fracturing of America*. New York: Scribner, 2008.

Pierpont, Claudia Roth. *Roth Unbound: A Writer and His Books*. New York: Farrar, Straus and Giroux, 2013.

Podhoretz, Norman. "The Adventures of Philip Roth," *Commentary*, October 1998, https://www.commentarymagazine.com/articles/norman-podhoretz/the-adventures-of -philip-roth/.

Posnock, Ross. *Philip Roth's Rude Truth: The Art of Immaturity*. Princeton: Princeton University Press, 2006.

Pozorski, Aimee. "Philip Roth's Biography." In *Critical Insights: Philip Roth*, edited by Aimee Pozorski, 25–42. Pasadena: Salem Press, 2013.

———. *Roth and Trauma: The Problem of History in the Later Works (1995–2010)*. New York: Bloomsbury: 2011.

Remnick, David. "Philip Roth's Propulsive Force." *New Yorker*, June 4 & 11, 2018, https://www.newyorker.com/magazine/2018/06/04/philip-roths-propulsive-force.

———. "Philip Roth Says Enough." *New Yorker*, November 9, 2012, https://www.newyorker.com/books/page-turner/philip-roth-says-enough?reload=true.

Rothstein, Mervyn. "Philip Roth and the World of 'What If?'" In *Conversations with Philip Roth*, edited by George Searles, 198–201. Jackson: University of Mississippi Press, 1992.

Royal, Derek Parker. "Pastoral Dreams and National Identity in *American Pastoral* and *I Married a Communist*." In *Philip Roth: New Perspectives on an American Author*, edited by Derek Parker Royal, 185–207. Westport: Praeger Publishers, 2005.

Rushdie, Salman. "How Philip Roth Became a Political Prophet." *The Forward*, October 3, 2018, https://forward.com/culture/411296/salman-rushdie-how-philip-roth-became-a-political-prophet/.

Said, Edward. *On Late Style: Music and Literature Against the Grain*. New York: Random House, 2006.

Schuessler, Jennifer. "Philip Roth Says He Has Given His Last Public Reading." *The New York Times*, May 9, 2014, https://www.nytimes.com/2014/05/10/books/philip-roth-says-he-has-given-his-last-public-reading.html.

Scott, A.O. "In Search of the Best." *New York Times*, May 21, 2006, https://www.nytimes.com/2006/05/21/books/review/scott-essay.html.

Shechner, Mark. *Up Society's Ass, Copper!: Rereading Philip Roth*. Madison: University of Wisconsin Press, 2003.

Shiffman, Dan. "*The Plot Against America* and History Post-9/11." *Philip Roth Studies* 5.1 (2009): 61–73.

Shipe, Matthew. "After the Fall: The Terror of History in Philip Roth's *Indignation*," *Philip Roth Studies* (Spring 2018): 1–24.

———. "*Exit Ghost* and the Politics of Late Style." *Philip Roth Studies*. 5.2 (Fall 2009): 43–58.

———. "Life." In *Philip Roth in Context*, edited by Maggie McKinley, 9–18. Cambridge: Cambridge University Press, 2021.

———. "Twilight of the Superheroes: Philip Roth, Celebrity and the End of Print Culture." In *Roth and Celebrity*, edited by Aimee Pozorski, 101–18. Lanham: Lexington Books, 2012.

Shostak, Debra. "Introduction: Roth's America." In *Philip Roth: American Pastoral, The Human Stain, The Plot Against America*, edited by Debra Shostak, 1–14. New York: Continuum Books, 2011.

———. *Philip Roth—Countertexts, Counterlives*. Columbia: University of South Carolina Press, 2004.

———. "Roth and Gender." In *The Cambridge Companion to Philip Roth*, edited by Timothy Parrish, 111–26. Cambridge: Cambridge University Press, 2007.

Skidelsky, William. "*The Humbling* by Philip Roth." Review of *The Humbling*, by Philip Roth. *The Observer*, October 25, 2009, https://www.theguardian.com/books/2009/oct/25/the-humbling-philip-roth-skidelsky.

Taylor, Ben. *Here We Are: My Friendship with Philip Roth*. New York: Penguin Books, 2020.

Trilling, Diana. "The Uncomplaining Homosexuals." *Harper's Magazine*, August 1969, https://harpers.org/archive/1969/08/the-uncomplaining-homosexuals/.

Updike, John. "Recruiting Raw Nerves." Review of *Operation Shylock*, by Philip Roth. In *More Matter: Essays and Criticism*, 291–99. New York: Fawcett Books, 1999.

———. "Wrestling to be Born." Review of *The Counterlife*, by Philip Roth. In *Odd Jobs: Essays and Criticism*, 373–80. New York: Alfred A. Knopf, 1991.

———. "Yahweh over Dionysus, in Disputed Decision." Review of *The Anatomy Lesson*, by Philip Roth. In *Odd Jobs: Essays and Criticism*, 366–72. New York: Alfred A. Knopf, 1991.

Witcombe, Mike. "In the Roth Archives: The Evolution of Philip Roth's Kepesh Trilogy." *Philip Roth Studies* 13.1 (2017): 45–63.

Wood, James. "My Hero: Philip Roth." *The Guardian*, March 22, 2013, https://www.theguardian.com/books/2013/mar/22/my-hero-philip-roth-james-wood.

———. "The Unceasing Necessity of Philip Roth." *New Yorker*, May 23, 2018, https://www.newyorker.com/books/page-turner/the-unceasing-necessity-of-philip-roth.

Yardley, Jonathan. "Homeland Insecurity." Review of *The Plot Against America*, by Philip Roth. *Washington Post*, October 3, 2004, http://www.washingtonpost.com/wpdyn/articles/A63751-2004Sep30.html.

INDEX

influences, 7–8; literary themes, 2–3; marriage to Claire Bloom, 14, 98; marriage to Margaret "Maggie" Martinson Williams, 13, 21, 36–37, 77; Newark, 9–10; patriotism, 7; performance, 6; politics, 4–6, 7, 21, 32–33; relationship with brother, 8; relationship with parents, 8–9; psychoanalysis, 21; retirement, 18; sexuality, 60; Weequahic neighborhood, 9–10; writing process, 16
Roth, Philip (character), 3, 78–83, 109–11
Roth, Sanford "Sandy," 8, 40
Royal, Derek Parker, 17
Rubin Jerry, 90
Rushdie, Salman, 19, 105
"Ruthless Intimacy of Fiction, The," 7, 86

Sabbath, Mickey (character), 55, 85–88, 91, 96, 103
Sabbath's Theater, 16–17, 82, 84–88, 102, 116, 118; history, 87–88; National Book Award, 84; realism, 87
Said, Edward, 3, 56, 112–13
Salinger, J. D., 24–25; The Catcher in the Rye, 24
Schulz, Bruno, 14
Scott, A. O., 85
Second World War, 3, 6–7, 18, 21, 25, 34, 40, 67, 85, 87, 93, 99–100, 106, 108–9, 117
September 11, 2001, attacks, 5, 57, 107, 114
sexuality: in The Anatomy Lesson, 51; in The Breast, 63–64; in The Dying Animal, 70–74; in Exit Ghost, 57; in The Ghost Writer, 42; in "Goodbye, Columbus" 24–24; in "On the Air," 34; in The Professor of Desire, 65–66; in Portnoy's Complaint, 29–31; in When She Was Good, 28
sexual revolution, 14; in The Breast, 63; in The Dying Animal, 70–72 in Kepesh trilogy, 59; in Portnoy's Complaint, 30–31
sexual trauma, 126n19; in When She Was Good, 28
Shechner, Mark, 67, 80

Shop Talk, 81
Shostak, Debra, 37, 54, 59, 72–73, 85, 122n10, 124n2
Sidon, Karel, 14
Silent Generation, 17
Simic, Charles, 115
Simon, David, 19
Skidelsky, William, 116
Smilesburger, 82
Smith, Bessie, 71
Sontag, Susan, 20
Sosa, Sammy, 102
Spielvogel, Otto, 14, 29, 32–33, 37, 74
Stempel, Herb, 46
Swift, Jonathan, 63; Gulliver's Travels, 63

Tarnopol, Peter (character), 14, 36–37, 39, 41, 58, 98
Taylor, Benjamin 90, 98; Here We Are, 108
Tet offensive, 92, 126m16
Thoreau, Henry David, 101
Tolstoy, Leo, 66; War and Peace, 47
Trilling, Diana, 31
Trump, Donald, 7, 18–19
Twain, Mark, 7
Twenty-One (television quiz show), 46

Umanoff, Marcia, 51, 95–96
University of Chicago, 12, 21, 36, 40, 50, 82
University of Iowa's Writer's Workshop, 13
University of Pennsylvania, 13
Updike, John, 2, 6, 20, 26, 46–46, 56, 81, 124n11, 125n2; Couples, 30, 46; In the Beauty of the Lilies, 17; Rabbit Angstrom tetralogy, 41

Vietnam War, 7, 21, 88, 90; in American Pastoral, 91–93; in The Anatomy Lesson, 49; in Our Gang, 35; in Portnoy's Complaint, 32; in Zuckerman Unbound, 47

Watergate, 35, 50, 92, 95
Weather Underground, 70, 89–90, 92–93, 126n16